T0123484

An Analysis of

Jacques Derrida's

Structure, Sign and Play in the Discourse of the Human Sciences

Tim Smith-Laing

Published by Macat International Ltd
24:13 Coda Centre, 189 Munster Road, London SW6 6AW.

Distributed exclusively by Routledge
2 Park Square, Milton Park, Abingdon, Oxon OX14 4RN
711 Third Avenue, New York, NY 10017, USA

Routledge is an imprint of the Taylor & Francis Group, an informa business

www.macat.com
info@macat.com

Cataloguing in Publication Data
A catalogue record for this book is available from the British Library.
Library of Congress Cataloguing-in-Publication Data is available upon request.
Cover illustration: Jonathan Edwards

ISBN 978-1-912453-52-8 (hardback)
ISBN 978-1-912453-07-8 (paperback)
ISBN 978-1-912453-22-1 (e-book)

Notice
The information in this book is designed to orientate readers of the work under analysis,
to elucidate and contextualise its key ideas and themes, and to aid in the development
of critical thinking skills. It is not meant to be used, nor should it be used, as a
substitute for original thinking or in place of original writing or research. References and
notes are provided for informational purposes and their presence does not constitute
endorsement of the information or opinions therein. This book is presented solely for
educational purposes. It is sold on the understanding that the publisher is not engaged
to provide any scholarly advice. The publisher has made every effort to ensure that
this book is accurate and up-to-date, but makes no warranties or representations with
regard to the completeness or reliability of the information it contains. The information
and the opinions provided herein are not guaranteed or warranted to produce particular
results and may not be suitable for students of every ability. The publisher shall not be
liable for any loss, damage or disruption arising from any errors or omissions, or from
the use of this book, including, but not limited to, special, incidental, consequential or
other damages caused, or alleged to have been caused, directly or indirectly, by the
information contained within.

CONTENTS

THE MACAT LIBRARY

The Macat Library is a series of unique academic explorations of seminal works in the humanities and social sciences – books and papers that have had a significant and widely recognised impact on their disciplines. It has been created to serve as much more than just a summary of what lies between the covers of a great book. It illuminates and explores the influences on, ideas of, and impact of that book. Our goal is to offer a learning resource that encourages critical thinking and fosters a better, deeper understanding of important ideas.

Each publication is divided into three Sections: Influences, Ideas, and Impact. Each Section has four Modules. These explore every important facet of the work, and the responses to it.

This Section-Module structure makes a Macat Library book easy to use, but it has another important feature. Because each Macat book is written to the same format, it is possible (and encouraged!) to cross-reference multiple Macat books along the same lines of inquiry or research. This allows the reader to open up interesting interdisciplinary pathways.

To further aid your reading, lists of glossary terms and people mentioned are included at the end of this book (these are indicated by an asterisk [*] throughout) – as well as a list of works cited.

Macat has worked with the University of Cambridge to identify the elements of critical thinking and understand the ways in which six different skills combine to enable effective thinking.
Three allow us to fully understand a problem; three more give us the tools to solve it. Together, these six skills make up the **PACIER** model of critical thinking. They are:

ANALYSIS – understanding how an argument is built
EVALUATION – exploring the strengths and weaknesses of an argument
INTERPRETATION – understanding issues of meaning

CREATIVE THINKING – coming up with new ideas and fresh connections
PROBLEM-SOLVING – producing strong solutions
REASONING – creating strong arguments

To find out more, visit **WWW.MACAT.COM.**

CRITICAL THINKING AND "STRUCTURE, SIGN, AND PLAY IN THE DISCOURSE OF THE HUMAN SCIENCES"

Primary critical thinking skill: INTERPRETATION
Secondary critical thinking skill: REASONING

"Structure, Sign, and Play in the Discourse of the Human Sciences" is a superb example of the skills of interpretation and reasoning. In particular it shows how they can be used in combination to unpick and remake arguments. The subject of Derrida's essay is meaning itself—the central issue of interpretative critical thinking—and he chooses to investigate it by interpreting the idea of interpretation itself. Looking at the foundational ideas of the school of thought known as structuralism, he zooms in on issues of terminology to expose fundamental contradictions within structuralist thought. He produces his strongest proofs of those contradictions through careful interpretation of structuralist texts themselves. On close inspection, those texts reveal inescapable contradictions that undercut their conclusions. Insistently exposing the cross-currents of meaning within these texts allows Derrida to turn to his reasoning skills and build a strong, persuasive argument for a way of proceeding that accepts structuralist approaches, but moves through them towards a different way of thinking about truth and interpretation.

ABOUT THE AUTHOR OF THE ORIGINAL WORK

Jacques Derrida (1930–2004) was one of the most influential philosophers and literary theorists of the twentieth century. Born to a Jewish–Algerian family in the French colony of Algeria in 1930, his early experiences of cultural dislocation helped inform a career spent exposing the problems and possibilities of meaning in our world. Derrida spent the bulk of his career teaching in France, with visiting posts in the United States. His career took off in the late 1960s with the groundbreaking books *Of Grammatology* and *Writing and Difference*, which helped him become one of the world's most famous, and most controversial, philosophers.

ABOUT THE AUTHOR OF THE ANALYSIS

Dr Tim Smith-Laing took his DPhil in English literature at Merton College, Oxford, and has held positions at Jesus College, Oxford, and Sciences Po in Paris.

ABOUT MACAT

GREAT WORKS FOR CRITICAL THINKING

Macat is focused on making the ideas of the world's great thinkers accessible and comprehensible to everybody, everywhere, in ways that promote the development of enhanced critical thinking skills.

It works with leading academics from the world's top universities to produce new analyses that focus on the ideas and the impact of the most influential works ever written across a wide variety of academic disciplines. Each of the works that sit at the heart of its growing library is an enduring example of great thinking. But by setting them in context – and looking at the influences that shaped their authors, as well as the responses they provoked – Macat encourages readers to look at these classics and game-changers with fresh eyes. Readers learn to think, engage and challenge their ideas, rather than simply accepting them.

'Macat offers an amazing first-of-its-kind tool for interdisciplinary learning and research. Its focus on works that transformed their disciplines and its rigorous approach, drawing on the world's leading experts and educational institutions, opens up a world-class education to anyone.'

Andreas Schleicher,
Director for Education and Skills, Organisation for Economic
Co-operation and Development

'Macat is taking on some of the major challenges in university education ... They have drawn together a strong team of active academics who are producing teaching materials that are novel in the breadth of their approach.'

Prof Lord Broers,
former Vice-Chancellor of the University of Cambridge

'The Macat vision is exceptionally exciting. It focuses upon new modes of learning which analyse and explain seminal texts which have profoundly influenced world thinking and so social and economic development. It promotes the kind of critical thinking which is essential for any society and economy.
This is the learning of the future.'

Rt Hon Charles Clarke, former UK Secretary of State for Education

'The Macat analyses provide immediate access to the critical conversation surrounding the books that have shaped their respective discipline, which will make them an invaluable resource to all of those, students and teachers, working in the field.'

Professor William Tronzo, University of California at San Diego

WAYS IN TO THE TEXT

KEY POINTS

- Jacques Derrida was an influential French theorist known for his contributions to the schools of "deconstruction"* and "poststructuralism."*

- "Structure, Sign, and Play" posits that knowledge in the world cannot be anchored to stable origins, but is subject to radical "play."*

- "Structure, Sign, and Play" remains one of the most influential and controversial texts in modern thought.

Who Was Jacques Derrida?

Jacques Derrida, the author of "Structure, Sign, and Play in the Discourse of the Human Sciences," was an influential French philosopher born in Algeria in 1930. Educated in French schools in Algeria, he went on to study at one of France's most prestigious universities, the École Normale Supérieure (ENS),* a center for French intellectual life. Getting into the ENS allowed Derrida to work under and alongside some of the most important French thinkers of the twentieth century, such as Roland Barthes* and Michel Foucault.* Derrida later went on to teach there for twenty years, during which time he came to be ranked among the most influential philosophers in the world.

Derrida became well known in the late 1960s, when he published a number of groundbreaking books and essays. These works, including "Structure, Sign, and Play in the Discourse of the Human Sciences" (1966) examined the foundations of human language and knowledge. Derrida's work exposed what he saw as fundamental problems with our understanding and use of language. In particular, Derrida sought to expose the ways in which both knowledge and meaning are built on the shaky foundations of language, which is always shifting.

Derrida's ideas were controversial, and he had many strong critics, but the possibilities his work opened up were considered revolutionary by many, especially in the field of literary studies. There he helped found the influential movements of deconstruction and poststructuralism. From the 1980s onwards, he was one of the most famous philosophers in the world. While teaching in France and the United States, he wrote nearly 100 books before his death from cancer in 2004.

What Does "Structure, Sign and Play" Say?

"Structure, Sign, and Play in the Discourse of the Human Sciences" argues that meaning and human knowledge cannot be securely anchored and made certain in or through language. This is a complex idea that comes out of Derrida's understanding of a school of thought known as "structuralism."*

Structuralism worked on the basis that words are only related to reality by linguistic conventions. There is, for instance, no actual link between the word "book" and a real book except for the fact that English-speakers use that word to refer to that kind of object. To think of it another way, the word "book" can only mean what it means to us because of its place in the "structure" of English as a whole language, and our familiarity with that structure.

Most importantly, we know that "book" has a *different* meaning from other words, and this, in fact, is how we know "book" refers to the kind of object it does. We know it does not mean the same as "paper," "pamphlet," "block," "scroll," and so on, because it is, in various ways, different from all of them. Our knowledge of English allows us to understand how it differs from those words, and so to understand each other when we say or write it. Because of this, structuralism argues, all meaning comes from webs of difference.

Structuralism applied this insight to understanding how meaning is generated in many different areas of human life and thought. It was dedicated to understanding how meaning was made, and how it can be understood, and to finding the fundamental structures that allow these things to occur. From the 1940s onwards, in the "human sciences"*—subjects ranging from literature to anthropology, philosophy, and sociology—structuralism became an important school of thought.

Derrida's essay exposes a contradiction in structuralism's desire to find *fundamental* structures. A fundamental structure, Derrida argues, would provide a sort of fixed point in an overall structure: an origin or center. This origin or center would, in turn, provide a kind of security to the overall production of meaning through difference. Derrida pointed out that this would help anchor or fix meaning—something he saw structuralists as being eager to do. A center or origin, by being fundamental, would not itself be subject to interpretation or gain meaning through difference, and so it would limit the flexibility or, as he calls it, the "play" of meaning in the whole structure, limiting interpretation and the possibility of meaning.

The problem Derrida saw was that this idea of a center or origin was itself in direct contradiction with structuralist thought. Because structuralism worked on the basis that language has no fixed relation to reality, no language can be fixed forever. And this, by definition, rules out the idea of a fixed center. Derrida argues that this contradiction can only be resolved by accepting that there is no center or origin, and that meaning cannot be completely fixed. Instead, it is always subject to play. Though the paper accepts that this might be a puzzling or even "monstrous" idea, Derrida argues that accepting the constant play of meaning is the only way to continue with philosophy.

Why Does "Structure, Sign and Play" Matter?

"Structure, Sign, and Play" had an enormous impact on thought across the humanities. It was very quickly seen as a revolutionary essay that had the potential to radically change critical approaches to language and meaning. Out of it, and the other works Derrida published in the next decade, grew two of the most important schools of thought in modern literary theory: deconstruction and the more generalized school of poststructuralism. Deconstruction pursued Derrida's technique of tracing the contradictions within texts through close reading, drawing from such readings deeper insights into the nature of language and literature. Poststructuralism, which includes deconstruction as a technique, would go on to apply Derrida's insights right across the range of the human sciences. Both schools of thought were particularly influential in the 1980s, and continue to produce new and challenging work today.

At the same time, the nature of Derrida's work means that it was also considered deeply controversial. Almost immediately after the essay appeared, Derrida found opponents both within and beyond structuralism. From the first presentation of the essay in 1966 right up to his death in 2004, Derrida was often accused of seeking to undermine the very ideas of knowledge and meaning themselves. His fiercest opponents saw the idea of "freeplay"* put forward in "Structure, Sign, and Play" as leading to a slippery slope in which nothing could be fixed or known for certain—from language right up to morality and ethics. Many critics also argued that Derrida's difficult writing style disguised a lack of real insight and acted as a protection against academic debate. These controversies continue right into the present, making Derrida still a vital point of knowledge for students wishing to understand debates around knowledge and meaning in our world.

For students of literature, "Structure, Sign, and Play" is an extremely powerful text that troubles some of our most basic assumptions about language and meaning. Though challenging, it also serves as a condensed summary of ideas that even today remain a subject of fierce debate in universities across the world. "Structure, Sign, and Play" has had a great deal of influence in literary studies, partially because at heart it is a text about reading. Derrida's main philosophical method is to read texts with an eye to seeing how they undermine themselves, and how they generate meanings other than those their authors intend. This is the technique at the heart of deconstruction, and one that is still used across the field of literary studies.

SECTION 1
INFLUENCES

MODULE 1
THE AUTHOR AND THE
HISTORICAL CONTEXT

KEY POINTS

- "Structure, Sign and Play" offered a radical account of human knowledge that still challenges thinkers today.

- "Structure, Sign and Play" was directly influenced by the radical thinkers Derrida knew in 1960s Paris.

- "Structure, Sign and Play" is marked by Derrida's suspicion of easy certainties—traceable to his roots in French Algeria.

Why Read This Text?

Jacques Derrida's "Structure, Sign and Play in the Discourse of the Human Sciences" is a watershed text in the history of literary theory and philosophy. Few essays can claim to have had as seismic an effect on modern thought as "Structure, Sign and Play"—the text that announced Derrida's arrival as a philosopher on the world stage.[1]

It is hard to overstate Derrida's importance as an influence in university departments across the world, in literature, philosophy, and beyond. As literary critic and theorist Derek Attridge* noted after Derrida's death, "Virtually every area of humanistic scholarship and artistic activity in the latter part of the 20th century" felt his influence.[2]

Though the essay itself, and Derrida's work in general, can be challenging, familiarity with his ideas reveals them as clear and more logical than they might first seem. For literary scholars, too, Derrida is valued not just for the earthquake he helped set off in literary theory, but for his own literary qualities as a writer. "Structure, Sign and Play"

> 66 Ah, you want me to say things like 'I-was-born-in-El Biar-on-the-outskirts-of-Algiers-in-a-petty-bourgeois-family-of-assimilated-Jews-but ...' Is that really necessary? I can't do it. 99
>
> Jacques Derrida, Interview, 1983

is a literary text in its own right: an enduring classic of literary-theoretical writing, in the fullest sense of the term.

Author's Life

Jacques Derrida was born Jackie Derrida in Algiers, Algeria, July 5, 1930, the third child of Georgette Safar and Aimé Derrida.[3] Algeria was a French colony, and as part of the country's Jewish community the Derridas—unlike other Algerians—held full French citizenship.[4] As such, Derrida spoke French, and was educated under the French system.

Despite early missteps, Derrida was an ambitious student. In 1949 he gained a place at the prestigious Lycée Louis-le Grand* in Paris to study for entrance to the École Normal Supérieure (ENS)—one of France's most prestigious educational institutions. He entered the ENS in 1952 and would return to teach there from 1964–1984.

During the mid-1960s, Derrida associated with a new generation of groundbreaking French intellectuals, and his reputation began to grow. He came to wider attention in 1966 with the presentation of "Structure, Sign and Play" at Johns Hopkins University,* Baltimore. The next year he published three books, *Speech and Phenomena*,[5] *Of Grammatology*,[6] and *Writing and Difference* (containing "Structure, Sign and Play").[7] These confirmed his place as one of France's foremost philosophers, and with English translations following from the mid-1970s onward, that prominence spread abroad.

The works that followed—"in excess of 100 volumes" by one count[8]—placed Derrida at the heart of debates surrounding "theory." While his work reverberated through universities across the world, critics accused him of writing in an overly difficult style. When he died of pancreatic cancer in 2004, he remained one of the world's most famous philosophers, not least for the supposed difficulty of his work as summed up in a front-page *New York Times* headline "Jacques Derrida, Abstruse Theorist, Dies in Paris at 74."[9]

Author's Background

Derrida was reluctant to link his life and work in straightforward terms, though much of his writing contains memoir.[10] It is, however, possible to trace a line between his life and his writing's dominant themes: dislocation, rupture, and paradoxical positioning inside *and* outside of systems.

As a Jewish Algerian, Derrida lived at the crossroads of three identities: Jewish (though non-observant), French (though Algerian and Jewish), and Algerian (though French). The conflict between these identities was more confusing for the young Derrida because of his inability to separate them or to comprehend why others did. Writing about his exclusion from school in 1942 under the anti-Semitic policies of Vichy France,* he describes himself as "a little black and very Arab Jew who understood nothing about [his situation]" praying to God in "Christian Latin French."[11] His was a mixed, marginal position that contradicted divisions others saw as natural—a sensation central to "Structure, Sign and Play."

Language is crucial to Derrida, both biographically and thematically. Derrida's experience of French and Frenchness was marked by "brutal severance," between "French" and "French Algerians," and a "hand-to-hand combat with language in general."[12] The idea of linguistic severance and combat marks both "Structure, Sign and Play" and his entire career.[13]

NOTES

1   Jacques Derrida, *Writing and Difference,* trans. Alan Bass (London: Routledge, 2001), 351.

2   Derek Attridge and Thomas Baldwin, "Obituary: Jacques Derrida," *The Guardian,* 11 October, 2004, accessed March 2, 2018, https://www.theguardian.com/news/2004/oct/11/guardianobituaries.france

3   See Geoffrey Bennington and Jacques Derrida, *Jacques Derrida,* trans. Geoffrey Bennington (Chicago: University of Chicago Press, 1999), 325–336. The standard full-length biographical study is Benoît Peeters, *Derrida: A Biography*, trans. Andrew Brown (London: Polity, 2013).

4   See Leslie Hill, *The Cambridge Introduction to Jacques Derrida* (Cambridge: Cambridge University Press, 2007), 2.

5   Jacques Derrida, *La Voix et le Phénomène: introduction au problème du signe dans la phénoménologie de Husserl* (Paris: Presses Universitaires de France, 1967); *Speech and Phenomena and Other Essays on Husserl's Theory of Signs*, trans. David B. Allison, Newton Garver (Evanston: Northwestern University Press, 1973).

6   Jacques Derrida, *De la grammatologie* (Paris: Minuit, 1967); *Of Grammatology* (Corrected Edition), trans. Gayatri Chakravorty Spivak (Baltimore: Johns Hopkins University Press, 1998).

7   Jacques Derrida, *L'écriture et la différence* (Paris: Seuil, 1967).

8   Leslie Hill, *The Cambridge Introduction to Jacques Derrida* (Cambridge: Cambridge University Press, 2007), 1.

9   Jonathan Kandell, "Jacques Derrida, Abstruse Theorist, Dies at 74," *The New York Times*, October 10, 2004, 1.

10 See Geoffrey Bennington and Jacques Derrida, *Jacques Derrida,* (Chicago: University of Chicago Press, 1993), and Benoît Peeters, Derrida: A Biography, trans. Andrew Brown (London: Polity, 2013), 2–3.

11 Bennington and Derrida, *Jacques Derrida*, 58.

12 Jacques Derrida, *Monolingualism of the Other; or, The Prosthesis of Origin,* (Stanford: Stanford University Press, 1998), 46.

13 Derrida, *Monolingualism*, 46.

MODULE 2
ACADEMIC CONTEXT

KEY POINTS

- "Structure, Sign and Play" exists at the intersection of literary theory and the philosophy of the "human sciences."

- During the 1960s, French literary theorists and philosophers were heavily invested in the school known as "structuralism."

- Derrida was in certain ways an orthodox structuralist, but his work used structuralism to challenge its own foundations.

The Work In Its Context

Jacques Derrida's 1966 "Structure, Sign and Play in the Discourse of the Human Sciences" works across several fields. Though often read as literary theory, its concerns have to do with far broader methodological concerns in the "human sciences." That label, more commonly used in European than in Anglo-American institutions, covers the full set of the humanities and social sciences, but often with particular prominence given to linguistics,* anthropology, literature, and philosophy.

Within this field, "Structure, Sign and Play" concerns itself with the school of thought called "structuralism." Developing out of the work of early twentieth century Swiss linguist Ferdinand de Saussure,* structuralism had migrated successively into anthropology, philosophy, and literary theory until, in France in particular, it had come to dominate thought in the human sciences. By the 1960s, it was perhaps the most significant theoretical paradigm for the human sciences in continental Europe.

> ❝ Structuralism is not a new method; it is the awakened and troubled consciousness of modern thought. ❞
>
> Michel Foucault, *The Order of Things*

Despite its significance, however, structuralism was still often regarded as something of an *avant-garde* movement, whose validity remained to be assessed. It was with this in mind that the symposium "The Languages of Criticism and the Sciences of Man" at Johns Hopkins University was convened in 1966, with Derrida among the structuralist thinkers invited to explore and assess structuralism's impact on the human sciences.[1]

Overview Of The Field

Fundamentally, structuralism is a particular way of understanding the production of meaning. As a methodology, it stems directly from the ideas and terminology outlined by Saussure in his 1916 *Course in General Linguistics*.[2] Saussure's central interest was in how language—that is, all language—functions as a system, and how it produces and communicates meaning.[3]

For Saussure, the basic unit of language is the "sign,"* which, in turn, is composed of two inseparable elements: the "signifier"* (the word or "sound-image") and the "signified"* (the concept linked to that "sound-image"). For instance, the word "arbor" in Latin is a *signifier* for the *signified* that English-speakers identify with "tree." Saussure's crucial contention is that the signifier-signified relationship in every sign is *arbitrary*; that is, there is no intrinsic link between words and concepts.[4] "Tree" and "arbor" are both only tied to the concept *tree* by conventions within English and Latin.

In this model, those words call up the concept *tree* only through their place in the structures of those languages.[5] Because there is nothing tying signifiers and signifieds together except these structures, all meaning stems from the ways in which signs form webs of difference and similarity within these structures.[6] English-speakers, for instance, know that the sign "tree" is different from the sign "car" (whose signified is inanimate), less different from the sign "cat" (whose signified has life, but of a different kind), similar to the sign "plant" (the same kind of life, but generalized), and very like the sign "shrub" (same kind of life, less generalized), *et cetera*. These webs of difference, maintained by conventions of use, define signs such that meaning can be generated and communicated between those familiar with English.

Saussure noted that this insight applied across the human sciences to any area where meaning was at issue. For his own part, he suggested the foundation of what he termed *semiology*:* "A science that studies the life of signs within society." That is to say, a discipline studying how "signs" operate not just in spoken or written language, but in all the activities that communicate meaning in human societies. It is out of this foundation that structuralism as a more general methodology beyond linguistics appeared.

Academic Influences

Derrida was an omnivorous philosophical and theoretical reader, and, as Edward Baring has noted, "was not the protégé of a particular school."[7] In "Structure, Sign and Play" alone it is possible to highlight important influences in philosophy—including the German philosophers Friedrich Nietzsche* and Martin Heidegger*[8]—and psychology—above all Sigmund Freud,* the Austrian founder of psychoanalysis—as well as Saussure.[9] However, the key thinkers for understanding the logic of "Structure, Sign and Play" are the structuralists who followed Saussure.

First among these is the French anthropologist Claude Lévi-Strauss* who, as Derrida put it in the essay, weighed "heavily on the contemporary theoretical situation."[10] From the mid-1940s onwards, Lévi-Strauss used Saussure's insights to elaborate what he termed "structural anthropology."* Structural anthropology examined the production of meaning across the full range of human behavior, from social organization, to mythology, and even to food preparation. Structural anthropology worked on the basis that the make-up of human minds and human cultures stems directly from elementary thought structures that create patterns of difference. These fundamental patterns, Lévi-Strauss argued, can be traced within all cultures, no matter the surface differences between them.

Lévi-Strauss became a towering figure in French thought and was crucial to structuralism's spread across the human sciences. And though Derrida noted that the idea of "structure" is "as old as Western science and Western philosophy," he nevertheless regarded structural*ism*, and Lévi-Strauss's work in particular, as marking an "event" in Western thought. That is to say, he believed that consciously analyzing the relationship between structure and meaning was a new and significant departure. It is that "event" that forms the crux of "Structure, Sign and Play."[11]

NOTES

1   See Richard Macksey and Eugenio Donato, eds. *The Structuralist Controversy: The Languages of Criticism and the Sciences of Man* (Baltimore: Johns Hopkins University Press, 1972), xv.

2   See Joanne A. Hsu, "Saussure" in *The Encyclopedia of Literary and Cultural Theory*, ed. Gregory Castle, Robert Eaglestone, and M. Keith Booker (Chichester: Wiley-Blackwell, 2011), 420pp, and Ferdinand de Saussure, *Course in General Linguistics*, ed. Charles Bally and Albert Sechehaye, trans. Wade Baskin (New York: The Philosophical Library, 1959).

3   Ferdinand de Saussure, *Course in General Linguistics*, ed. Charles Bally and Albert Sechehaye, trans. Wade Baskin (New York: The Philosophical Library, 1959), 1–5.

4   Saussure, *Course in General Linguistics*, 67.

5   Saussure, *Course in General Linguistics*, 67.

6   Saussure, *Course in General Linguistics*, 115.

7   Edward Baring, *Young Derrida and French Philosophy, 1945–1968*
     (Cambridge: Cambridge University Press, 2011), 2–3.

8   See François Dosse, *History of Structuralism, Volume I: The Rising
     Sign, 1945–1966*, trans. Deborah Glassman (Minneapolis: University of
     Minnesota Press, 1997), 364–79.

9   *Of Grammatology* (Corrected Edition), trans. Gayatri Chakravorty Spivak
     (Baltimore: Johns Hopkins University Press, 1998).

10   Jacques Derrida, "Structure, Sign and Play in the Discourse of the Human
     Sciences," in *Writing and Difference*, trans. Alan Bass (London: Routledge,
     2001), 357.

11   Derrida, "Structure, Sign and Play," 351.

THE PROBLEM

KEY POINTS

- Both in France and the United States, academics were trying to assess the meaning and impact of structuralism for critical enquiry.

- Structuralism seemed to hold up the possibility of a new way of analyzing the production of meaning across all human activities.

- Derrida questioned the radicalism of structuralism and sought to pursue its ideas to their furthest conclusions.

Core Question

The core question of Jacques Derrida's "Structure, Sign and Play in the Discourse of the Human Sciences" is what would happen if theorists followed the logic of structuralism through to its furthest conclusions. This, though, must be seen in the context of a time when neither the basic nature of structuralism nor its full implications were apparent. Indeed, at base, Derrida's paper should be read in relation to the two more basic questions: "What is structuralism?" and "What can it do for criticism?"

These are, in certain ways, the core unanswered questions of structuralism itself, which despite its vast impact in the humanities and social sciences never coalesced into a unified "school of thought." Indeed, as literary theorist Jonathan Culler* notes, beyond its basic concern with "the structures that produce meaning," structuralism remains almost impossible to define in the singular.[1] Never locked into a settled form, it is perhaps best seen as, in Derrida's own words, a "frenzy of experimentation" rather than a movement.[2]

> **❝** What Americans call poststructuralism existed even
> before the structural paradigm waned. In fact, it was
> contemporary with its triumph. **❞**
>
> François Dosse,* *History of Structuralism*

It was with this instability in mind that "The Languages of
Criticism and the Sciences of Man" colloquium was convened. By
inviting some of the most prominent structuralist thinkers of the time
to contribute to a unified program of papers and debates, the literary
critic Eugenio Donato* and his colleague Richard Macksey* hoped
to outline both the nature of structuralism and the possibilities it
might hold for methodologies in the human sciences.

The Participants

Though Macksey and Donato admitted the impossibility of
"marshaling under a single flag" the speakers they had invited, their
program represented a veritable "Who's Who" of structuralism.[3] With
the exceptions of the anthropologist Claude Lévi-Strauss and the
philosopher-historian Michel Foucault, almost all the major
proponents of structuralist thought were present. Among the most
significant structuralist figures included were René Girard,* Lucien
Goldmann,* Jacques Lacan* and Roland Barthes—thinkers whose
disparate disciplinary backgrounds, approaches, and objects of study
show how varied structuralism itself was.

Girard was a philosopher, anthropologist, and historian. During the
mid- to late-1960s, he was known above all for using structuralist ideas
of difference to found his theories on religion, desire, and *mimesis**
(imitation). He would later distance himself from structuralism.
Goldmann, meanwhile, was a Marxist* philosopher and sociologist
who combined Marxist theories of historical change with structuralist
methodologies to form what he termed "genetic structuralism."*

Lacan—who would emerge as one of the most famous and most controversial figures in literary and psychoanalytical theory—was a psychoanalyst who had incorporated recognizably structuralist models of language into his understanding of the unconscious. He had already become one of the most influential and controversial theorists in France. Barthes, finally, was a self-identified "semiotician," following up on Saussure's projected "sciences of signs." A cultural and literary critic, he was a hugely significant figure in France, frequently seen as the leading light of the structuralist *nouvelle critique** ("new criticism").

The Contemporary Debate

Rather than arriving at a definitive stance on its core questions, the Johns Hopkins conference would instead become ground zero for "The Structuralist Controversy," which centered on two issues fundamental to Derrida's paper, highlighted by Macksey and Donato in their remarks in symposium proceedings. The first of these was the impact of relating all areas of the human sciences to a "*general theory* of signs and language systems." The second was "the question of 'mediations' between *objective and subjective judgments*" (author's italics).[4] These, in turn, came down to a central tension in structuralist discourse: the paradox of elaborating a "scientific" theory of meaning that rested on a fundamental assumption of arbitrary relations between signs and signifieds.

It is perhaps Girard and Goldmann's papers that point up this tension most clearly.[5] Girard's paper, "Tiresias* and the Critic" used the Greek myth of the tragic king Oedipus* and the blind soothsayer Tiresias to discuss the problem of the supposedly "ideal" objective interpreter. Structuralism's insight, Girard suggested, was to show that "objective" interpretations of fact neglected how facts come to have *significance*—that is, meaning for someone in a given context. In the myth, Oedipus is dedicated to knowledge as fact, with no interpretative sense of how it relates to him personally. The seer Tiresias, meanwhile, like the structuralist critic, understands the necessity of interpretation, and more particularly of "redoubling … interpretation upon itself."[6] He sees both the need to interpret, and to consider how interpretation works depending on the person, the context, and the method involved. Structuralism, in Girard's view, promised a science of interpreting interpretation.

Goldmann's stance was similar, but with a crucial difference. For him such a science would be useless unless its interpretations were grounded in solid historical reality. His paper, "Structure: Human Reality and Methodological Concept" took pains to outline a methodology that would root all structuralist insights within historical fact, and provide strict—though finally obscure—criteria for "satisfactory" interpretations.[7]

Goldmann's talk prompted a long discussion on the apparent contradiction between structuralism's aims and its fundamental tenets. On one hand, the project of structuralism was to elaborate what he termed a "scientific"—or factually objective—methodology for analyzing meaning.[8] On the other, to do so, it relied on Saussure's doctrine of the arbitrariness of sign—an axiom that seemed to dictate what Goldmann called "the impossibility of objectivity." The paradox would be central to Derrida's work.

NOTES

1   Jonathan Culler, *On Deconstruction: Theory and Criticism after Structuralism* (Ithaca NY: Cornell University Press, 1983), 21.

2   Jacques Derrida, *Writing and Difference,* trans. Alan Bass (London: Routledge, 2001), 5.

3   Richard Macksey and Eugenio Donato, eds. *The Structuralist Controversy: The Languages of Criticism and the Sciences of Man* (Baltimore: Johns Hopkins University Press, 1972), ix.

4   Macksey and Donato, eds. *The Structuralist Controversy,* xvi.

5   Roland Barthes, "Writing: an intransitive verb?" in Richard Macksey and
    Eugenio Donato eds. *The Structuralist Controversy: The Languages of
    Criticism and the Sciences of Man* (Baltimore: Johns Hopkins University
    Press, 1972), and Jacques Lacan, "Of Structure as an Inmixing of an
    Otherness Prerequisite to Any Subject Whatever," in Richard Macksey and
    Eugenio Donato, eds. *The Structuralist Controversy: The Languages of
    Criticism and the Sciences of Man* (Baltimore: Johns Hopkins University
    Press, 1972). See also Benoît Peeters, *Derrida: A Biography,* trans. Andrew
    Brown (London: Polity, 2013), 167.

6   René Girard, "Tiresias and the Critic," in Richard Macksey and Eugenio
    Donato, eds. *The Structuralist Controversy: The Languages of Criticism and
    the Sciences of Man* (Baltimore: Johns Hopkins University Press, 1972), 18.

7   Lucien Goldmann, "Structure: Human Reality and Methodological Concept,"
    in Richard Macksey and Eugenio Donato, eds. *The Structuralist Controversy:
    The Languages of Criticism and the Sciences of Man* (Baltimore: Johns
    Hopkins University Press, 1972), 104.

8   Goldmann, "Structure," 117.

THE AUTHOR'S CONTRIBUTION

KEY POINTS

- Derrida proposed that structuralism's conception of structure fundamentally destabilized the idea of fixed meaning.

- "Structure, Sign and Play" made a basic contradiction in structuralism clear, paving the way for the new paradigm of poststructuralism.

- Derrida's work grew directly out of the logical principles of structuralism and the work of Claude Lévi-Strauss.

Author's Aims

Jacques Derrida wrote "Structure, Sign and Play in the Discourse of the Human Sciences" in 1966. Its writing came in the middle of a period that saw him complete several works that aimed to critique structuralist thought from within. And it is in the context of Derrida's general aims in this fertile period—culminating in the publication of *Of Grammatology*, *Writing and Difference*, and *"Speech and Phenomena" and Other Essays on Husserl's Theory of Sign* in 1967—that the aims of "Structure, Sign and Play" should be understood. The paper is both just one small part of this project and its clearest, most concise expression.

As the literary theorist and translator of *Of Grammatology*, Gayatri Spivak,* has noted, "Derrida's criticism of 'structuralism,' even as he inhabits it, would be a sweeping one," related to the two core questions analyzed above: "the possibility of a general law," and "the possibility of objective description."[1] Written, according to Derrida himself, in just ten days, "Structure, Sign and Play" attempts to use the most basic axioms and logic of structuralism to argue for nothing

> ❝ There is more to do in interpreting interpretations than interpreting things, and more books upon books than on any other subject: all we do is gloss each other. ❞
>
> Michel de Montaigne,* "On Experience," in *Essays*

less than a complete reconsideration of the idea of "meaning." It does this by showing that the "general law" of structuralism itself precludes any possibility of "objectivity." Fundamentally, in his own words, Derrida's aim came down to replacing old approaches that dreamed of "deciphering a truth" with an interpretative approach that "affirms play and tries to pass beyond man and humanism."[2] In other words, it is an approach that accepts the unfixed, flexible status of both meaning and human nature, and seeks to produce interpretation with status in mind.

Approach

While Derrida's claims were both radical and new, the approach of "Structure, Sign and Play" consists, at least rhetorically, in revealing that these claims were already implicit in other theorists' works. From the outset, in fact, the essay presents itself as an explanation and interpretation of something that had already occurred, what Derrida termed in the essay's opening an "event," "a *rupture* and a redoubling" in the idea of knowledge.[3] As Benoît Peeters has noted, "It was a matter … not of moving on from philosophy, but of reading philosophers in a really new way."[4]

Derrida does this by performing these readings within "Structure, Sign and Play" itself. Having noted his now-famous "event," he moves on to suggest that it would be "naïve to refer to [it as] an event," or as the product of a particular "doctrine, or an author." Instead, he argues that it is implicit in several major figures in the history of Western thought: the nineteenth-century German philosopher Friedrich

Nietzsche, the twentieth-century German philosopher Martin Heidegger, and the early twentieth-century psychologist and psychoanalyst Sigmund Freud. Each of these figures, deeply influential on Derrida's thought, had, he suggested, radically unpicked the solid foundations of their specialism to produce something new. Nietzsche had critiqued the idea of eternal truths and fixed morals, Heidegger the idea of being, and Freud the idea of the stable, known self.

Finally, however, Derrida turns his attention to a single figure, dedicating the rest of "Structure, Sign and Play" to a series of close readings of Claude Lévi-Strauss. It is through Lévi-Strauss—the anthropologist whose work is most clearly responsible for the crossing over of structuralist thought from linguistics into the wider domain of the human sciences—that Derrida most directly uncovers and unravels the foundations of structuralism. It is this maneuver that most clearly represents Derrida's inventive turn as a philosopher and reader: his use of structuralism's principles, as expressed by their most venerable exponent, to move beyond structuralism.

Contribution In Context

"Structure, Sign and Play" is an extremely original piece that builds carefully on the work of other thinkers, and makes its debts clear throughout. Derrida was present at the 1966 conference, "The Languages of Criticism and the Sciences of Man," held at Johns Hopkins University, Baltimore, under the banner of structuralism, and it is very much as a structuralist—accepting its premises and with full knowledge of its major thinkers—that he spoke. He goes beyond this, however, to make clear his more general philosophical debts to the major figures in European thought named above. In some measure then, the young and still relatively unknown Derrida, was presenting himself as a reader and scholar of philosophy and structuralist theory, rather than as a radical intervener in its trajectory.

Thus, while "Structure, Sign and Play" presents itself as helping to mark a "rupture" in philosophical thought, the essay quite deliberately consists of borrowed ideas, and, indeed, seeks to foreground the borrowing of ideas as its central methodological premise. One of the paper's favored terms, *bricolage*,* acts as a kind of methodological pun on precisely this paradox of borrowing methods from old thinkers specifically to critique those thinkers' ideas.[5]

Bricolage has come to have increasingly specialized literary-theoretical uses, but it is also a French word for using whatever materials and techniques come to hand in order to get a job done. Its standard context in everyday use is in DIY, where it has connotations ranging from the semi-professional right down to what English-speakers might refer to as "jury-rigging" – that is, makeshift repairs from the materials at hand. It is, in turn, a term Derrida lifts directly from Lévi-Strauss's own work, as a means of unpicking its underlying, contradictory meanings.

NOTES

1   Gayatri Chakravorty Spivak, "Translator's Preface" in Jacques Derrida, *Of Grammatology*, trans. Gayatri Chakravorty Spivak (Baltimore: Johns Hopkins University Press, 1997), LVII.

2   Jacques Derrida, "Structure, Sign and Play in the Discourse of the Human Sciences," in *Writing and Difference*, trans. Alan Bass (London: Routledge, 2001), 369.

3   Derrida, "Structure, Sign and Play," 351.

4   Benoît Peeters, *Derrida: A Biography*, trans. Andrew Brown (London: Polity, 2013), 167–68.

5   Derrida, "Structure, Sign and Play," 360.

SECTION 2
IDEAS

MODULE 5
MAIN IDEAS

KEY POINTS

- Derrida's central aim was to reveal the contradiction at the heart of structuralism in order to open up a new mode of interpretation.

- Derrida's central argument was that structuralism, in contradiction with itself, continued to treat meaning as moored or centered.

- "Structure, Sign and Play" is a challenging text on account of its specialized vocabulary and embeddedness in structuralist discourse.

Key Themes

The key argument of Jacques Derrida's "Structure, Sign and Play in the Discourse of the Human Sciences" is that structuralism ignored its own most important insight. In Derrida's reading, by noting that meaning is produced only through webs of difference between signs, structuralism had definitively unmoored meaning from any anchoring "origin" or "center." This lack of origin or center logically dictates that meaning is not a *result* but a *process*, and the necessarily continuous interaction of signs in this process gives rise to meanings that are, therefore, always subject to possible shifts and reassessments. Meaning, therefore, is always in "play."

Despite this, Derrida argues, structuralist thinkers had tended to behave as if that play could be limited. They had persistently conjured or substituted artificial "centers" or "origins" to circumscribe it. However, by doing so, they were ignoring the precise notion on which structuralism relied—resulting in a doomed, self-contradictory

> ** The entire history of the concept of structure, before the rupture of which we are speaking, must be thought of as a series of substitutions of center for center. **
>
> Jacques Derrida, "Structure, Sign and Play in the Discourse of the Human Sciences"

pattern of thought.

Derrida's stance is that the structuralist opening up of play is indisputable. Structuralism, however, finds various methods of turning away from that insight and attempting to circumscribe play. Derrida offers two "interpretations of interpretation" in the face of this: either an impossible and "nostalgic" quest for centers that either do not exist or cannot be reclaimed, or a "joyous" recognition of the possibilities created by the lack of center.[1] It is the latter that he advocates, and which would become the basis of poststructuralism.

Exploring The Ideas

Derrida's argument works logically from two premises. The first is Ferdinand de Saussure's axiom of the arbitrariness of the sign—the idea that words are not intrinsically related to objects and concepts, but have meanings only within a whole system of language. Meaning, thus, rests on the relation of signs to signs, via webs of difference.[2] Crucially, there is no point of origin within these structures, no "center" to which everything can be related. Nothing in language, therefore, can escape or "transcend" difference.

The second premise is that this insight from linguistics applied to all fields where meaning was at stake—across the human sciences, to the study of mythology, or social conventions, ritual, literature, philosophy, and so on. Derrida marks this as "the moment when language invaded the universal problematic, when, in the absence of a center or origin, everything became discourse … that is to say, a system in which the central signified, the original or transcendental signified, is never absolutely present outside a system of differences."[3] Indeed, as he puts it, "The absence of the transcendental signified extends the domain and the play of signification infinitely."[4]

For Derrida, this is not an insight limited to structuralism. He sees the entire history of Western philosophy as a series of attempts to define a fixed "origin," a "center," or a "presence" on which to found itself. This, he suggests, can be seen clearly in the way "all the [philosophical] names related to fundamentals" have been attempts to fix "an invariable presence" as the foundation of meaning.[5] He notes, moreover, that these "substitutions of center for center" continue even among thinkers who logically accept the radical unmooring of meaning implicit in structuralism. Foremost among these is the structural anthropologist Claude Lévi-Strauss, whose work Derrida subjects to several close readings. Exposing Lévi-Strauss's serial attempts to offer temporary centers or presences, Derrida argues that his work, despite revealing time and again a *lack* of foundational center, acts "paradoxically, in complicity with that philosophy of presence."[6]

Derrida's key turn is to embrace the play opened up by the absence of any foundational origin, presence, or center. Whereas previous philosophers had tended to conceive of the absent center as "loss," about which to feel "saddened, *negative*, nostalgic, guilty," he determines instead to opt for "the joyous affirmation of the play of the world," an "affirmation of a world of signs without fault, without truth, and without origin."[7] This, he suggests, would be the foundation of a new philosophy, even if such a philosophy might appear to present-day philosophers as a "terrifying form of monstrosity."[8]

Language And Expression
"Structure, Sign and Play" is a dense text by a philosopher regularly ranked among the most challenging writers of the twentieth century.

The major hurdle for students and newcomers to literary theory is Derrida's assumption of readers' familiarity with both the basic ideas of structuralism and a wide range of specific writers.

It is helpful, but not indispensable, for instance, to have some sense of the writers who are key touchstones for Derrida, and whom he uses as shorthand for certain kinds of approach, particularly the eighteenth-century Swiss-born philosopher and novelist Jean-Jacques Rousseau* and the nineteenth-century German philosopher Friedrich Nietzsche. It is important, though, to recognize that it is possible to follow Derrida's arguments without following up such references—fundamentally, "Structure, Sign and Play" does not rely on them for its coherence.

More important is Derrida's use of specialized terms (e.g. *signifier, signified, episteme,* * *teleological,* * *eschatological**) and of everyday terms with specialized philosophical meanings (e.g. *sign, structure, center, presence*). The most vital of these are unpacked above and in the glossary to this analysis, but a useful general reference for readers fresh to Derrida's terminology is Niall Lucy's *Derrida Dictionary.*[9]

It is important, however, not to exaggerate Derrida's difficulty. Though famous for the density of his prose and the complexity of his arguments, "Structure, Sign and Play" works quite logically from the two basic premises outlined above. Readers who pay attention to this guiding logic will be able to follow Derrida's argument, and see how it leads to the essay's crux and conclusions.

NOTES

1   Jacques Derrida, "Structure, Sign and Play in the Discourse of the Human Sciences," in *Writing and Difference*, trans. Alan Bass (London: Routledge, 2001), 369.

2   See Module 2 and Ferdinand de Saussure, *Course in General Linguistics*, ed. Charles Bally and Albert Sechehaye, trans. Wade Baskin (New York: The Philosophical Library, 1959), 67.

3   Derrida, "Structure, Sign and Play," 354.

4   Derrida, "Structure, Sign and Play," 354.

5   Derrida, "Structure, Sign and Play," 353.

6   Derrida, "Structure, Sign and Play," 367.

7   Derrida, "Structure, Sign and Play," 369.

8   Derrida, "Structure, Sign and Play," 370.

9   Niall Lucy, *A Derrida Dictionary* (Oxford: Blackwell, 2004).

MODULE 6
SECONDARY IDEAS

KEY POINTS

- The main secondary idea of "Structure, Sign and Play" is that of "deconstruction;" the second is the notion of *bricolage*.

- "Deconstruction" as a key idea in poststructuralism had a vast impact on the humanities, while *bricolage* is a powerful tool for literary studies.

- "Deconstruction" has proven to be one of the most influential, and controversial, ideas in modern philosophy and literary theory.

Other Ideas

The most notable secondary idea in Jacques Derrida's "Structure, Sign and Play in the Discourse of the Human Sciences" is the concept of "deconstruction." Though Derrida never laid out a method of deconstruction as such, the term widely became synonymous with Derrida's work from the early 1970s onwards. And, within and alongside "poststructuralism," it went on to become one of the most significant literary-theoretical positions of the late twentieth century.[1]

Despite this, deconstruction remains, in John Coker's words, little more than a "provisional label" for "the various ways in which philosophical and literary texts are read by Derrida."[2] As the term itself indicates, these readings tend towards the breaking down of the texts in question. And, as the readings of Claude Lévi-Strauss in "Structure, Sign and Play" show, Derrida's favored approach is to read texts *against themselves*, by demonstrating how, unwittingly, they undermine their own positions.

> ❝ Language can only have been born in one fell swoop. Things could not have set about acquiring signification progressively ... a transition came about from a stage where nothing had a meaning to another where everything possessed it. ❞
>
> Claude Lévi-Strauss, *Introduction to the Work of Marcel Mauss**

The other secondary idea put forward in the paper is *bricolage*—a term that Derrida adapts from both Claude Lévi-Strauss and the structuralist literary critic Gerard Genette.* Taken originally from its use Lévi-Strauss's 1962 anthropological study *The Savage Mind*, *bricolage* essentially means the borrowing and adapting of whatever methods might seem productive for the reading of a text or the discussion of a problem. As will be seen, though, its significance for Derrida lies in the fact that it is both a specific form of philosophical and critical procedure, and a description of the inevitable nature of philosophy itself.

Exploring The Ideas

The word "deconstruction" appears just once in "Structure, Sign and Play" but has gone on—through Derrida's other works—to be perhaps the single most important theoretical concept associated with Derrida. The essay does not elevate it to the status of a proposed methodology, however; instead it simply proposes an unnamed mode of having "a critical relation to the language of the social sciences" and "critical responsibility."[3] This mode of reading, Derrida writes, "is a question of explicitly and systematically posing the problem of the status of a discourse which borrows from a heritage the resources necessary for the deconstruction of that heritage itself."[4]

That is to say that deconstruction consists of using the tools, methods, or language of a particular discipline or methodology in order to show up the limitations, blindspots, or contradictions of a text in that discipline or methodology. This is both a definition of deconstructive reading, and a description of "Structure, Sign and Play" itself, which draws from structuralism the seeds of structuralism's deconstruction. As Derrida noted in a later work, however, this should not be confused with *destructive* reading. Though he adapted it originally from German philosopher Martin Heidegger's *Destruktion*,* Derrida was keen to avoid any sense of "an annihilation or a negative reduction."[5] Deconstruction might instead be read as pulling texts apart in order to see that there is *more* occurring in them than their authors are aware of or can control.

This process is, as the theorist Gayatri Spivak has noted, linked to *bricolage*.[6] As a serious methodological procedure, *bricolage* is in fact a form of ironic joke, linked to the all-important Derridean concept of "play" (*jeu*). In *The Savage Mind*, Lévi-Strauss traces the verb *bricoler*'s origin to the realm of games (*jeux*)—"ball games, billiards, hunting, and horse-riding"—where it denotes unexpected movements or going off course. In the modern day, Lévi-Strauss notes, it has come to mean "to tinker," and the *bricoleur* is someone who is definitively amateur "who works with his hands, using means that, by comparison with those of the man of art, are devious [*détournés*]."[7] That verb, *détourner*, is also used in the sense of "to hijack," which is precisely what Derrida does to Lévi-Strauss's own structuralist tools and methods.

As Derrida notes, Gerard Genette takes *bricolage* as a nearly perfect description of criticism—in particular literary criticism—proposing it as a "fertile procedure" for any arena where language is at stake.[8] Genette's formulation, which describes Derrida's, is that *bricolage* is suited to any "discourse upon a discourse" or "meta-language."*[9] For Genette, literary criticism cannot escape or stand outside literature to comment upon it, and is, therefore, "meta-literature … a literature whose object is literature itself."[10] This "meta-language" status is crucial both to *bricolage* and to Derrida's whole relationship to philosophy. In the same way, Derrida suggests it is impossible to critique philosophy from *outside*, as there is nowhere outside the structure of knowledge/language. What one can do, however, is *bricoler* from philosophy the means for a meta-philosophy that could critique it.

Bricolage is, thus, closely linked to deconstruction. For Derrida, it is both a kind of anti-methodology methodology—which permits the user to act in non-methodical ways—and a description of the condition of all philosophy—which, whether it knows it or not, is doomed always to borrow and adapt its tools. Derrida's novel step is to discover in that condition a means of continuing to do philosophy.

Overlooked

Though "Structure, Sign and Play" is a rich, dense text, one can hardly describe any of its ideas as having been overlooked. They have, however, often been misconstrued, with Derrida's fiercest critics accusing him of pulling the rug out from under knowledge altogether. Deconstruction has been described as repudiating the idea of reality itself, and even milder critics have argued that by infinitely extending the field of play in the constitution of meaning, Derrida is anti-rationalist*—attacking the idea of reason itself.[11]

"Structure, Sign and Play" does not support these readings. The essay does critique philosophy's dreams of fully grasping the world as it is, but it does not take up an anti-rational or nihilistic* position. Instead, Derrida's tone is celebratory, arguing that readers (i.e. philosophers, anthropologists, literary critics) should see the opening up of "play" as a matter for "joyous affirmation." It is the beginning of a "*seminal* adventure"—which is to say, through the etymology of *seminal*, an adventure in which the "seeds" or fertility of meaning will reveal themselves.[12]

In other words, Derrida's arguments do not posit the impossibility of meaning, but the possibility of meaning. His work, despite the specialized nature of Derrida's language, deliberately opens the examination of meaning up to the casual tinkerer, the non-specialist *bricoleur.*

NOTES

1   François Cusset, *French Theory: How Foucault, Derrida, Deleuze, & Co. Transformed the Intellectual Life of the United States*, trans. Jeff Fort (Minneapolis: University of Minnesota Press, 2008), 107ff.

2   John Coker, "Jacques Derrida," in *The Blackwell Guide to Continental Philosophy*, ed. Robert Solomon and David Sherman (Oxford: Blackwell, 2003), 265.

3   Jacques Derrida, "Structure, Sign and Play in the Discourse of the Human Sciences," in *Writing and Difference*, trans. Alan Bass (London: Routledge, 2001), 356.

4   Derrida, "Structure, Sign and Play," 356–57.

5   Jacques Derrida, "Letter to a Japanese friend," in *Psyche: Inventions of the Other,* vol. 2, ed. Peggy Kamuf and Elizabeth Rottenberg (Stanford: Stanford University Press, 2007), 1–2.

6   Gayatri Chakravorty Spivak, "Translator's Preface," in Jacques Derrida, *Of Grammatology*, trans. Gayatri Chakravorty Spivak (Baltimore: Johns Hopkins University Press, 1997), xviii.

7   Claude Lévi-Strauss, *La Pensée sauvage* (Paris: Plon, 1962), 26 (author's translation); the full passage can be found in English in Claude Lévi-Strauss, *The Savage Mind*, trans. Anonymous (London: Weidenfeld and Nicolson, 1966), 17.

8   Gerard Genette, *Figures I* (Paris: Éditions du Seuil, 1966), 149 (author's translation).

9   Genette, *Figures I*, 146 (author's translation).

10 Genette, *Figures I*, 146 (author's translation).

11 See, e.g., Raymond Tallis, *Not Saussure. A Critique of Post-Saussurean Literary Theory,* (London: Macmillan Press, 1988), 188.

12 Derrida, "Structure, Sign and Play," 369.

MODULE 7
ACHIEVEMENT

KEY POINTS

• The deconstruction of structuralism carried out in "Structure, Sign and Play" was viewed almost immediately as unanswerable.

• The paper's presentation to an audience of prominent structuralists in the United States enabled its fast uptake in academia.

• The radical nature of Derrida's critique ensured both hostility and misunderstanding among many critics.

Assessing The Argument

Jacques Derrida's "Structure, Sign and Play in the Discourse of the Human Sciences" was soon greeted as a hugely significant intervention in contemporary philosophy and literary theory. Derrida's intention had been to draw his audience's attention to what he saw as a "rupture" already present in structuralist thought, and his paper was soon marked out as a persuasive argument for a change in theoretical approach.[1] This much was immediately evident to those in the paper's original audience. As he made clear in his concluding remarks to the symposium, the organizer, Richard Macksey, viewed it as one of the most "radical" of the papers given in its "reappraisals of our assumptions."[2]

Though, as will be seen below, "Structure, Sign and Play" has often attracted criticism from other philosophical schools and ideological stances, it is both clear and coherent within the premises Derrida adopts from structuralism. This is, perhaps, most notable in the close readings of Claude Lévi-Strauss's work that Derrida uses to illustrate

❝ Structuralism with its rarefied stakes ... was something that should be left behind in order to move toward a more playful poststructuralism. The word will not make its appearance until the beginning of the 1970s, but all the Americans present at Johns Hopkins in 1966 realized that they had just attended the live performance of its public birth. ❞

François Cusset,* *French Theory*

his main line of argument. Those readings show both a breadth of familiarity with Lévi-Strauss's work and a remarkable depth of engagement with it—both of which are reflected again in *Of Grammatology*, published the following year.[3] It is, above all, through its deconstruction of Lévi-Strauss's work that Derrida's critique of structuralism gains its force.

Despite its forceful argument, though, "Structure, Sign and Play" remains a deliberately open-ended paper. Notably, it does not offer any kind of positive critical program from its arguments. Having made his case for structuralism's internal contradictions, Derrida only goes so far as to point the way towards something *other* than structuralism; he does not say what it could or should be. Indeed, he states in his closing paragraph that he does "not believe that ... there is any question of choosing" which way to take.[4] He will only go so far as to say that "we are catching a glimpse" of "a kind of question," and something "unnamable which is proclaiming itself."[5]

Achievement In Context

"Structure, Sign and Play" has often been written into the history of literary theory as bringing about precisely the "rupture" and "event" that Derrida purported to describe. The idea that the paper was immediately greeted as a watershed in the history of criticism should, perhaps, not be overplayed. The record of the conversation directly following it shows a mixture of admiration, disagreement, and puzzlement at a striking paper given by someone who, as Derrida's biographer Benoît Peeters remarks, was both "young and unknown."[6] The most direct comments came from the Marxist structuralist Lucien Goldmann, who granted that Derrida's "criticism was remarkable," but "of a destructive character," and made clear his total disagreement with Derrida's stance.[7]

Despite this, as the implications of "Structure, Sign and Play" became clear, both the paper and the Johns Hopkins conference gained significance. With the proceedings published first in 1970, and then republished the following year under the new title *The Structuralist Controversy*, the conference became the first means by which many American readers encountered European literary theory and the implications it had for their work. Indeed, as François Cusset has noted, the symposium "The Languages of Criticism and the Sciences of Man" was "retrospectively" seen as "something of a founding event" in the history of what is known by the broad label of "French theory."*

The nature of that founding can be credited entirely to Derrida, whose paper was at the heart of what turned the symposium from an education in structuralism for American academics into a controversy that undermined the nature of structuralism itself. Thanks "Structure, Sign and Play," Cusset argues, "the conference that was supposed to present structuralism to Americans served rather to invent … its designated successor": poststructuralism. And though poststructuralism did not emerge fully until the early 1970s—thanks in large part to Derrida's work in the period immediately following the conference—no point marks its birth more clearly than the presentation of "Structure, Sign and Play" at Johns Hopkins on October 21, 1966.

Limitations

Some of the criticisms originally leveled at "Structure, Sign and Play" have dogged its reception ever since. Foremost among which is the charge of "destructiveness" made by Lucien Goldmann. Goldmann objected that Derrida's stance undermined criticism entirely by pointing out its "contradictory" postulates.[8] Derrida was quick to respond that "I was quite explicit about the fact that nothing of what I said had a destructive meaning," and to state that "*déconstruction* ... has nothing to do with destruction."[9] Somewhat defensively, he also responded to a criticism Goldmann had not in fact made, stating that he also believed in "the necessity of scientific work in the classical sense."[10]

In one form or another, however, both charges—that Derrida's work is destructive, and that it denies any possible relation between language and reality, even in natural science—have gone on to be running themes in criticism of Derrida's work. As will be seen in more detail below, these suspicions about his work have placed limits on Derrida's reach and persuasiveness within academia. Though he was himself always at pains to deny their validity—stating that his methodology involves only "being alert to the implications, to the historical sedimentation of the language which we use"—readers have often seen something more fundamentally destabilizing, and even malign, in it.[11]

Derrida himself anticipates this hostility and fear in "Structure, Sign and Play." As he notes at the end of the paper, the form of thought "proclaiming itself ... can do so ... only under the species of the nonspecies, in the formless, mute, infant, and terrifying form of monstrosity."[12] In other words, the philosophy he was proposing was by its very nature new and threatening. While he also stated that he could not see why "I should renounce or why anyone should renounce the radicality of a critical work under the pretext that it risks the sterilization of science, humanity, progress, the origin of meaning, etc.," he nevertheless clearly understood that his radical critique might threaten readers' most fundamental assumptions.[13]

NOTES

1   Jacques Derrida, "Structure, Sign and Play in the Discourse of the Human Sciences," in *Writing and Difference*, trans. Alan Bass (London: Routledge, 2001), 351.

2   Richard Macksey and Eugenio Donato, eds. *The Structuralist Controversy: The Languages of Criticism and the Sciences of Man* (Baltimore: Johns Hopkins University Press, 1972), 320.

3   Jacques Derrida, *De la grammatologie* (Paris: Minuit, 1967); *Of Grammatology* (Corrected Edition), trans. Gayatri Chakravorty Spivak (Baltimore: Johns Hopkins University Press, 1998).

4   Derrida, "Structure, Sign and Play," 370.

5   Derrida, "Structure, Sign and Play," 370.

6   Benoît Peeters, *Derrida: A Biography*, trans. Andrew Brown (London: Polity, 2013), 167.

7   Macksey and Donato, eds., *The Structuralist Controversy*, 270.

8   Macksey and Donato, eds., *The Structuralist Controversy*, 270.

9   Macksey and Donato, eds., *The Structuralist Controversy*, 270–71.

10   Macksey and Donato, eds., *The Structuralist Controversy*, 271.

11   Macksey and Donato, eds., *The Structuralist Controversy*, 271.

12   Derrida, "Structure, Sign and Play," 370.

13   Macksey and Donato, eds., *The Structuralist Controversy*, 271.

PLACE IN THE AUTHOR'S WORK

KEY POINTS

- Derrida's *œuvre* focuses on the way in which meaning and certain forms of knowledge are inevitably contingent.*

- "Structure, Sign and Play" is a relatively early work that marks the point where Derrida began to be noticed as a significant thinker.

- "Structure, Sign and Play" helped announce Derrida's significance, but his reputation was cemented by longer works from the same period.

Positioning

In a number of ways 1966's "Structure, Sign, and Play in the Discourse of the Human Sciences" is the piece that most clearly marks the transition from Jacques Derrida's early work to his philosophical maturity. Though Derrida himself was quick to deny any sense of completion or coming together when asked about his work in the period, 1966–1967 undoubtedly marks the point at which his career took off.[1] First, the presentation of "Structure, Sign and Play" at Johns Hopkins in 1966 publicly marked him out as a significant and radical voice in philosophy and theory. Then, the following year, that position was confirmed in France by the publication of his first three books—*Voice and Phenomenon*, *Of Grammatology*, and *Writing and Difference* (containing "Structure, Sign and Play").

Though Derrida's output from the 1970s right through to the early 2000s was prodigious, his reputation rests to a considerable degree on the insights of *Of Grammatology* and *Writing and Difference*. Similarly, though Derrida's thinking and writing ranged widely

> ❝ So none of this looks like a blossoming or a completeness, but rather like impromptus, fits and starts that, precisely because of their incompleteness and non-coincidence … induced me to continue. ❞
>
> Jacques Derrida, *A Taste for the Secret*

during his later career—from the nature of translation and the idea of the archive to mourning, friendship, and animality—his entire *oeuvre* is underpinned by the insights concerning language, meaning, and interpretation that he reached in the period surrounding "Structure, Sign, and Play." First among these is the notion that meaning is in the most radical sense *contingent*—that is, it is always subject to the possibility of change and can never be completely fixed. In this sense, though it does not anticipate every one of his later themes or every terminological contribution that Derrida would go on to make, "Structure, Sign and Play" continues to have a central place in Derrida's overall philosophical project.

Integration

Derrida's output was vast, to the point that some 14 years after his death, volumes of previously unpublished work are still in the process of being edited for publication. The major continuing project is the editing and translation of Derrida's seminars, appearing first in French with Editions Galilée, then in English via the Derrida Seminars Translation Project.[2] His current bibliography has been estimated at approximately 100 volumes, covering a considerable variety of topics.[3] But, as Derrida's friend and translator Geoffrey Bennington* has noted, his whole career can be pinned to unpicking the implications of a single, "simple" insight. This insight, as Bennington notes, is that "Identities in general (of whatever kind, at whatever level) arise out of difference, but difference is not itself any identity or indeed any thing at all. It is not that there are first things, and then differences and relations between them: the 'things' emerge only from the differences and relations, which have an absolute priority, and that emergence is never complete."[4]

From this basis, Bennington notes, comes "Derrida's simple claim … nowhere, ever, is there anything simple."[5] It is from this that the key concepts and terms of Derrida's career as a whole—play and freeplay, *différance*,* and logocentrism*—are drawn. Though simple, as Bennington argues, Derrida's insight has "almost unimaginably, fractally complex implications," and it is in exploring these in different contexts that Derrida pursued his philosophical and literary-theoretical enquiries.[6] With this in mind, despite the wide variety of topics that he considered across his career, Derrida's *oeuvre* can be seen as a coherent whole—much of which returns to the conception of meaning articulated in "Structure, Sign, and Play."

At the same time, however, Derrida himself clearly saw his career in terms of what one might, following Bennington, call fractal coherence: as a continuing project both of clarifying what he had said, and of continually branching out from it. Looking back on his work in particular, in 2001 he noted that it was precisely the "incompleteness" of *Writing and Difference* and *Of Grammatology* that made him continue working, "in part because I wanted to prevent misunderstandings" and in part in order "to prolong the non-coincidence"—the diverse nature and diverse subject matter—of his writings.[7]

Significance

"Structure, Sign and Play" is a short paper from a long career, but nevertheless holds a distinguished place in Derrida's work, both historically and philosophically. On the historical side, as has been noted above, the paper marked a watershed in the history of literary theory by publicly commencing the passage from structuralism to poststructuralism. And, as only the second of Derrida's essays to be published in English translation, in 1970, it was also one of the first chances Anglophone audiences had to encounter Derrida's work.[8] Philosophically, too, "Structure, Sign and Play" was a significant turning point for theorists in America; as Peeters notes, "In a few powerful paragraphs, the whole programme of deconstruction was set out"—a program that would have a vast impact on literary theory in the United States over the next two decades.[9]

At the same time, however, "Structure, Sign and Play" does not stand alone. It is, fundamentally, a summary piece, written by Derrida's own testimony in just 10 days in the run up to its presentation, explaining and illustrating ideas he had already forged elsewhere.[10] It is, thus, perhaps best seen as a superb condensation of ideas elaborated more fully across the essays collected in *Writing and Difference* as a whole, and in the more designedly coherent *Of Grammatology*. It is in the context of these two books, first translated into English in 1978 and 1976 respectively, that "Structure, Sign and Play" should be read, and thanks to their uptake in American theory during the 1980s that it has come to have the significance it has today.

NOTES

1   See, e.g., Jacques Derrida and Maurizio Ferrari, *A Taste for the Secret*, trans. Giacomo Donis, ed. Giacomo Donis and David Webb (London: Polity, 2001), 29.

2   Derrida's seminars, Editions Galilée, accessed March 2, 2018, http://www.editions-galilee.fr/f/index.php?sp=livAut&auteur_id=1902, (French), Derrida Seminars Translation Project, accessed March 2, 2018, http://derridaseminars.org/volumes.html (English).

3   Leslie Hill, *The Cambridge Introduction to Jacques Derrida* (Cambridge: Cambridge University Press, 2007), 1.

4   Geoffrey Bennington, "Embarrassing Ourselves," *Los Angeles Review of Books*, March 20, 2016, accessed March 2, 2018, https://lareviewofbooks.org/article/embarrassing-ourselves/#

5   Bennington, "Embarrassing Ourselves."

6   Bennington, "Embarrassing Ourselves."

7   Derrida and Ferrari, *A Taste for the Secret*, 30.

8   Derrida's first English publication was "The Ends of Man" in *Philosophy and Phenomenological Research* 30.1 (1969): 31–57.

9   Benoît Peeters, *Derrida: A Biography*, trans. Andrew Brown (London: Polity, 2013), 167–68.

10   François Cusset, *French Theory: How Foucault, Derrida, Deleuze, & Co. Transformed the Intellectual Life of the United States*, trans. Jeff Fort (Minneapolis: University of Minnesota Press, 2008), 30.

SECTION 3
IMPACT

THE FIRST RESPONSES

KEY POINTS

- Along with Derrida's other works, "Structure, Sign and Play" has been criticized for its difficulty, and accused of relativism* and even nihilism.

- The most hostile responses came from analytical philosophers,* accusing Derrida of attacking knowledge with pseudophilosophy.*

- Derrida's reception was centrally shaped by his uptake among literary critics, above all the so-called "Yale School."*

Criticism

It is difficult to disentangle the positive and negative responses to "Structure, Sign, and Play in the Discourse of the Human Sciences" from the reception given to Jacques Derrida's work in general over the course of the 1970s, 1980s, and 1990s. This difficulty stems predominantly from three circumstances.

The first of these is the near-simultaneous French publication in 1967 of *Writing and Difference* (in which "Structure, Sign and Play" was included) with *Speech and Phenomena* and *Of Grammatology*. It was on the basis of all three books that Derrida's reputation burgeoned, with reviewers responding to all three, rather than lending particular attention to "Structure, Sign, and Play."[1]

The second defining circumstance is the lag imposed by the translation of Derrida's work into English. Though "Structure, Sign and Play" was first published in English in 1970 as part of the conference proceedings,[2] *Writing and Difference* did not appear in

> **❝ I was wondering myself if I know where I am going. So I would answer you by saying, first, that I am trying, precisely, to put myself at a point so that I do not know any longer where I am going. ❞**
>
> Jacques Derrida, "Discussion" in *The Structuralist Controversy*

English until 1978.[3] *Speech and Phenomena* was translated in 1973, with *Of Grammatology* following in 1976. By the time *Writing and Difference* appeared, *Of Grammatology* had already taken up the position—which it would hold from then on—of being seen as Derrida's major programmatic work in the United States.[4]

The third, and perhaps most important, defining circumstance was the polarization of opinion concerning Derrida in the United States. Thanks to coverage in the important journal *Diacritics* in particular,[5] his US reputation was already both significant and controversial by the early 1970s. But the lack of translations often focused debate on a loose idea of what Derrida stood for rather than on specific texts. This has, in one way or another, shaped his reception ever since.

Responses

It is hard to overstate the polarization around Derrida's work in the Anglophone sphere. Nowhere is this clearer than in the so-called "Affaire Derrida" of 1992, when Cambridge University proposed awarding Derrida an honorary doctorate for his vast impact on contemporary thought. Protests from conservative professors at the university were reinforced by an open letter to *The Times* from 18 eminent philosophers.[6] The letter, composed by Barry Smith,* accused Derrida of employing "a written style that defies comprehension" to launch "semi-intelligible attacks upon the values of reason, truth, and scholarship."[7]

The Cambridge scandal was the culmination of critiques of Derrida and of the phenomenon of deconstruction that had gathered strength across the 1970s and 1980s in direct proportion to the positive reception that both received in certain university departments at the time. As François Cusset notes, along with Derrida himself, deconstruction became "the most bankable product ever to emerge on the market of academic discourses."[8] During the 1980s in particular, prominent critics and literary theorists, including Paul de Man,* J. Hillis Miller,* and Jonathan Culler promoted deconstruction as *the* new wave of literary thought.[9] By the mid-1990s, it had become so prominent that it could even be found referenced in the title of the Woody Allen* film *Deconstructing Harry* (1997).[10]

In certain quarters, it was precisely this popularity that led to suspicion. Though Derrida was awarded the Cambridge honorary degree in 1992, many remained unconvinced that his work was anything more than a passing fashion. At the core of their suspicion lay the difficulty of Derrida's writing style and his apparent undermining of objective knowledge. Despite Derrida's own denials, the eminent analytical philosopher John Searle*—echoing many others—maintained that deconstruction was an attack on "the concern with truth, rationality, logic, and 'the word' that marks the Western philosophical tradition,"[11] and that Derrida's writing was marked by "systematic evasiveness" of provable assertions.[12]

Conflict And Consensus

Though Derrida's importance to literary theory can hardly be contested, no real consensus has been reached between his detractors and defenders. On one hand his ideas have inspired some of the main currents in modern literary theory, including both deconstruction and poststructuralism, alongside major theorists such as Culler, de Man, Miller, and others. On the other hand, Derrida remained the subject of attacks from his detractors throughout the 1990s and beyond.

In 1996 the physicist Alan Sokal* used "Structure, Sign and Play" as a key reference in a hoax aimed at exposing what he saw as the fraudulence of poststructuralist theory. Sokal submitted a paper to the theoretical journal *Social Text* purportedly applying Derrida and other poststructuralist philosophers' work to "quantum gravity."[13] After the journal published the paper, Sokal revealed the hoax, arguing that it showed much theory—and the editors' understanding of it—to be "Fashionable Nonsense."[14] The hoax, and Sokal's follow-up book, generated such significant publicity that Derrida himself felt the need to respond directly. In the pages of the major French newspaper *Le Monde*, he called the hoax "sad," and denied any charges of "relativism" or of attacking scientific "reason."[15]

As can be seen in the caustic obituaries published in *The New York Times* and *The Economist* after Derrida's death in 2004, such attacks never quite faded.[16] The very hostility displayed by such major publications, though, makes clear that whatever some thought of him, Derrida remained one of the most significant and influential thinkers of the late twentieth century.

NOTES

1   See, e.g., Denis Saint-Jacques, "Jacques Derrida, *La Voix et le Phénomène*," Paris, P.U.F., Collection «Épiméthée», 1967; *L'Écriture et la différence*, Paris, Seuil, Collection «Tel Quel», 1967; *De la grammatologie*, Éditions de Minuit, Collection «Critique», 1967; *Études littéraires* 1, no. 3 (1968): 452–55.

2   In Richard Macksey, and Eugenio Donato, ed., *The Languages of Criticism and the Sciences of Man* (Baltimore: Johns Hopkins University Press, 1970); subsequently reprinted as *The Structuralist Controversy: The Languages of Criticism and the Sciences of Man* (Baltimore: Johns Hopkins University Press, 1972), with further reprints in 1975, 1977, 1979.

3   In the translation still used today: Jacques Derrida, *Writing and Difference*, trans. Alan Bass (London: Routledge, 2001).

4   See François Cusset, *French Theory: How Foucault, Derrida, Deleuze, & Co. Transformed the Intellectual Life of the United States*, trans. Jeff Fort (Minneapolis: University of Minnesota Press, 2008), 109–12.

5   Alexander Gelley, "Form as Force," *Diacritics* 2, no. 1 (1972): 9–13; Richard
     Klein, "Prolegomenon to Derrida." *Diacritics* 2, no. 4 (1972): 29–34, and
     Jacques Derrida, G Scarpetta, and J. L. Houdebine "Interview: Jacques
     Derrida," *Diacritics* 2, no. 4 (1972): 35–43; and Jacques Derrida and J.-L.
     Houdebine. "Interview: Jacques Derrida," *Diacritics* 3, no. 1 (1973): 33–46.

6   Barry Smith and Jeffrey Sims, "Revisiting the Derrida Affair with Barry
     Smith," *Sophia* Vol. 38 no 2, 1999, September–October: 142–70.

7   Barry Smith *et al*, "Letter," *The Times* (London). Saturday, May 9, 1992.

8   Cusset, *French Theory*, 107.

9   *On Deconstruction* (Ithaca, NY: Cornell University Press, 1982).

10   Cusset, *French Theory*, Ch. 5, and Benoît Peeters, *Derrida: A Biography*,
     trans. Andrew Brown (London: Polity, 2013), 451–61.

11   John R. Searle, "The Word Turned Upside Down," *The New York Review of
     Books*, October 27, 1983, accessed March 2, 2018, http://www.nybooks.
     com/articles/archives/1983/oct/27/the-word-turned-upside-down/.

12   John R. Searle, "An Exchange on Deconstruction," *The New York Review of
     Books*, February 2, 1984, accessed March 2, 2018, http://www.nybooks.
     com/articles/archives/1984/feb/02/an-exchange-on-deconstruction/.

13   Alan Sokal, "Transgressing the Boundaries: Towards a Transformative
     Hermeneutics of Quantum Gravity," *Social Text*, 46/47, Spring/Summer
     (1996): 217–52.

14   See Alan Sokal and Jean Bricmont, *Fashionable Nonsense: Postmodern
     Intellectuals' Abuse of Science* (New York: Picador 1998).

15   Jacques Derrida, "Sokal et Bricmont ne sont pas sérieux," *Le Monde*,
     November 20, 1997, 17.

16   Jonathan Kandell, "Jacques Derrida, Abstruse Theorist, Dies at 74," *The
     New York Times*, October 10, 2004; Anonymous, "Obituary: Jacques
     Derrida," *The Economist*, October 21, 2004.

MODULE 10
THE EVOLVING DEBATE

KEY POINTS

- "Structure, Sign and Play" helped birth poststructuralism, one of the most important theoretical movements of the late twentieth century.

- Poststructuralism challenges assumptions about knowledge, language, and human nature, emphasizing their contingency and freeplay.

- "Structure, Sign and Play" influenced major poststructuralists, including Paul de Man, and Judith Butler.*

Uses And Problems

Though Jacques Derrida's "Structure, Sign, and Play in the Discourse of the Human Sciences" was by no means specifically literary in its outlook or concerns, it was among literary critics and theorists that Derrida's ideas initially found the greatest uptake. Across the 1970s and 1980s, they would be at the core of the linked critical and philosophical movements known as deconstruction and poststructuralism.

Derrida's uptake as a "literary theorist" can be traced both to the fertile implications of his work for language and writing for literary scholars, and to the specific audience present at the presentation of "Structure, Sign, and Play." Among those present were the American literary critics, J. Hillis Miller and Paul de Man, who would both play important roles in applying Derrida's work to literature. As de Man noted in an interview on the topic, Derrida's "relative success" among literary critics can also be attributed to his basic attentiveness to texts and

> ❝ While it was not entirely clear what poststructuralism really amounted to, it had a veneer of danger that attracted and repelled in equal amounts. That it is now another academic badge that can be worn on the scholarly kitbag ... means that it is simply another 'ism' in a long list. ❞
>
> Benoît Dillet, Ian MacKenzie and Robert Porter, *The Edinburgh Companion to Poststructuralism*

textuality, and his use of "close reading" as the basis of his theories—techniques familiar to American students.[1] At the same time, however, Derrida's work appeared as both new and, crucially, "subversive"—something de Man noted as attractive to students at the time.[2]

For opponents of Derrida, that subversiveness was a central problem—part of what de Man would term *The Resistance to Theory*. At its heart, "Structure, Sign and Play" demanded a total reconsideration of how disciplines in the human sciences approached their own assumptions, their goals, and the status of the knowledge they aimed to produce—a position elaborated across *Writing and Difference* and *Of Grammatology*. As de Man characterized it, critics saw this—incorrectly—as "pure verbalism ... a denial of the reality principle."[3] For the distinguished critic Walter Jackson Bate* (quoted by de Man), Derrida's arguments amounted to "a nihilistic view of literature, of human communication, and of life itself."[4] In other words, rather than opening up literature and criticism, his critics saw Derrida's views as annihilating them altogether.

Allied to this objection was the persistent charge of obscurity, which has always dogged Derrida's work. Even those who promoted Derrida's work from the outset have often been inclined to accept its "monstrous difficulties," and they have been a central theme for critics like Bate.[5] Though occasionally exaggerated, the difficulty of Derrida's writing is undeniable. It presents considerable challenges to fluent readers of French, and—as Geoffrey Bennington has noted—occasionally generates insurmountable challenges for translators.[6]

Schools Of Thought

Miller and de Man directly aided the development of Derrida's ideas into a recognizable "school": deconstruction.[7] Both went on to teach at Yale University, where Derrida also lectured from 1975 onward, making the department a focal point for deconstruction. The "Yale School of Deconstruction" became a recognizable force in American literary studies from the turn of the decade, with the Yale anthology *Deconstruction and Criticism* (1979) proving an influential touchstone. Miller and de Man also directly influenced other scholars instrumental in Derrida's dissemination: Alan Bass,* the translator of *Writing and Difference*, was a student of Miller, while Gayatri Spivak*, the translator of *Of Grammatology*, was a former student of de Man.[8]

The second, linked, movement for which "Structure, Sign and Play" proved foundational is poststructuralism. A broad, complex, and flexible school of thought, poststructuralism is difficult to define, and is occasionally used interchangeably with deconstruction.[9] Fundamentally, however, poststructuralist thought extends Derrida's insights into "freeplay" as a means of questioning whether any element of human behavior or culture can be said to be truly "natural" or fixed—a central theme in poststructuralist discussions of politics and gender.

Crucially, however, Derrida is far from the sole thinker whose work has been influential on poststructuralism. Several of his contemporaries in France are also touchstones for contemporary poststructuralists—including the critic and semiotician Roland Barthes, the psychoanalyst and theorist Jacques Lacan, and perhaps most importantly, the historian and philosopher Michel Foucault. Together with Derrida these thinkers have coalesced into the broad, disparate corpus often referred to simply as "French Theory."[10]

In Current Scholarship

Since the 1980s, poststructuralism has continued to exert a strong influence over modern scholarship in a number of areas, with thinkers drawing both directly on Derrida's work, and on the broader corpus of "French Theory". Among Derrida's most prominent inheritors today are his translator Gayatri Spivak and the celebrated philosopher and theorist Judith Butler.

Spivak first rose to prominence with her long, theoretical preface to her translation of *Of Grammatology*—a preface which is itself a foundational text for deconstruction in the United States. She later consolidated her reputation with the famous 1983 essay "Can the Subaltern* Speak?"[11] Spivak has described herself as a "practical deconstructionist feminist Marxist," marking out her use of Derrida for practical, political ends. Her work expands on Derrida's critique of language, meaning, and knowledge by applying it—alongside other "French Theory"—to the situations of oppressed or "subaltern" people, in particular women and the subjects of colonial* rule.

Judith Butler, meanwhile, is perhaps the most influential inheritor of Derrida's thought today. A key exponent of "French Theory" as applied to feminist thought, Butler became one of the most famous philosophers in the world with *Gender Trouble* (1990).[12] The book applies poststructuralist thought to questioning the naturalness of gender and sexual identities, conveying insights that, though reliant on many thinkers, can be traced directly to Derrida's unpicking of structuralist assumptions in "Structure, Sign, and Play."

NOTES

1   Paul de Man, *The Resistance to Theory* (Minneapolis: University of Minnesota Press, 1986), 116.

2   De Man, *Resistance to Theory*, 117.

3   De Man, *Resistance to Theory*, 11.

4   De Man, *Resistance to Theory*, 22.

5   Richard Klein, "Prolegomenon to Derrida." *Diacritics* 2, no. 4 (1972), 29.

6   See Geoffrey Bennington, "Embarrassing Ourselves," *Los Angeles Review of Books*, March 20, 2016, accessed March 2, 2018, https://lareviewofbooks. org/article/embarrassing-ourselves/#, *passim.*

7   J. Hillis Miller, "Derrida and de Man: Two Rhetorics of Deconstruction," in Zeynep Direk and Leonard Lawlor, ed. *A Companion to Derrida* (Oxford: Blackwell, 2014).

8   Benoît Peeters, *Derrida: A Biography*, trans. Andrew Brown (London: Polity, 2013), 227.

9   Benoît Dillet, Ian MacKenzie and Robert Porter ed., *The Edinburgh Companion to Poststructuralism* (Edinburgh: Edinburgh University Press, 2013).

10 See, e.g., François Cusset, *French Theory: How Foucault, Derrida, Deleuze, & Co. Transformed the Intellectual Life of the United States*, trans. Jeff Fort (Minneapolis: University of Minnesota Press, 2008).

11 Revised and reprinted in Gayatri Chakravorty Spivak, *A Critique of Postcolonial Reason: Toward a History of the Vanishing Present* (Cambridge MA: Harvard University Press, 1999).

12 Judith Butler, *Gender Trouble: Feminism and the Subversion of Identity* (London: Routledge, 1999).

IMPACT AND INFLUENCE TODAY

KEY POINTS

- "Structure, Sign and Play" is regarded as a watershed in the history of literary theory and a seminal text in the history of ideas.

- The radical arguments in "Structure, Sign and Play" are still viewed with suspicion by those seeking a firm foundation for fixed knowledge.

- Derrida's inheritors have, often contentiously, extended the paper's arguments across the whole domain of life, society, and politics.

Position

Somewhat ironically for a text whose central argument concerns the impossibility of tracing origins, Jacques Derrida's "Structure, Sign, and Play in the Discourse of the Human Sciences" has guaranteed its place in intellectual history by appearing as an origin itself. Indeed, Derrida's own statement that an "event" had occurred has come to be seen as a self-fulfilling prophecy by marking the birth of poststructuralism.

Though by no means the sole text behind poststructuralism, there is no branch of poststructuralist thought—on everything from literature, to gender and sexuality, to politics, sociology, and even animal welfare—that cannot be traced back to the arguments outlined in "Structure, Sign, and Play." Along with a select few other French Theorists, Derrida lies at the heart of modern poststructuralism's persistent concern with deconstructing apparent truths and theories of truth. A 2009 survey of the most cited authors in the humanities for

> **❝** One can imagine Derrida as very modest, entirely occupied by reading and re-reading his predecessors with minute attention [or] as immodesty itself, forcing these same old texts to say something quite different from what they had always seemed to say ... Derrida is the object of simultaneous adulation and denunciation on both sides of this imagination, on both sides of the Atlantic. **❞**
>
> Geoffrey Bennington, *Jacques Derrida*

2007 showed both that poststructuralism was the dominant paradigm for research in the field, and that French Theory was its most important point of reference. Derrida was the third most cited author of the year, just behind the historian-philosopher Michel Foucault and the sociologist Pierre Bourdieu.[*1]

Precisely because of this, however, both "Structure, Sign and Play" and Derrida's thought more generally remain sites of strong contention and antipathy. The continuing suspicion that the arguments put forward in "Structure, Sign and Play" attack and undermine all areas of human reasoning—from scientific knowledge, to communication, to moral and ethical reasoning—remains strong. While some of the heat surrounding Derrida's place in the 1996 "Sokal Hoax"* has died down, the debates surrounding his theories still smolder on.

Interaction

As Sarah Wood has noted, it is extremely difficult to come to terms with Derrida's influence, even in terms of considering just a single piece of his work—be it a single essay, such as "Structure, Sign, and Play," or the collection in which that essay appears, *Writing and*

Difference. "The connections," Wood states "… are too many, too nuanced, too concerned with opening up reading and thought, to be reduced to a programme."[2] Indeed, Derrida's vast influence across the fields of the human sciences today has meant that his ideas have often been diffused to the point that what is referenced is not a specific book or paper, but rather an idea or figure called "Derrida." That, in turn, as the influential feminist philosopher Judith Butler has noted, is often closely bound up with the "curious American construction" called "French Theory."[3]

Butler is herself perhaps the foremost philosopher visibly continuing Derrida and the other French Theorists' project of calling into question the fundamental categories of thought and knowledge through their relation to language. In her seminal 1990 book *Gender Trouble*, "Structure, Sign and Play" is a tacit, but continuous presence, credited with marking the "poststructuralist break" upon which Butler's theory of gender depends.[4] Speaking more generally in a 2004 tribute to Derrida in the *London Review of Books*, Butler remarked that he "not only taught us how to read, but gave the act of reading a new significance and a new promise."[5] In her case, that promise has involved turning the tools of poststructuralism towards emancipatory political purposes.

Butler is perhaps the most visible Derridean scholar of the present day. Along with Gayatri Spivak, she is at the forefront of turning Derrida's insights on "the act of reading" towards increasingly political and emancipatory ends: the discussion of gender identity and gender inequalities, the analysis of ethnic, national or class identities and inequalities. Notably, Spivak and Butler collaborated on an updated fortieth anniversary edition of *Of Grammatology*.[6] To take Butler's term of preference, Derrida's insights, building on the "event" of "Structure, Sign and Play" can be a persistent and useful source of "trouble" for our assumptions regarding not just language and knowledge, but the nature of human existence itself.

The Continuing Debate

Derrida's potential to "trouble" our assumptions has at the same time been a continuous source of criticism against his work. From the 1980s, polemics against both Derrida himself and poststructuralism more generally (often used interchangeably with "postmodernism"), were continuous, both in and outside of academia.

These polemics, from the conservative philosopher Raymond Tallis's* 1988 *Not Saussure*,[7] to Barry Smith's 1992 open letter in *The Times* against Derrida's honorary Cambridge doctorate,[8] have continued right up to the present day. As recently as September 2017, the renowned American magazine *Atlantic Monthly* ran a cover story picking out poststructuralism as a crucial influence on the so-called "post-truth" era of politics. The article, titled, "How America Lost Its Mind," picked out "postmodern intellectuals—post-positivists, poststructuralists, social constructivists, post-empiricists, epistemic relativists, cognitive relativists, descriptive relativists" as "useful idiots" whose work had contributed directly to a decline in American intellectual and political values.[9]

Derrida made multiple attempts to clarify that he had never, in fact, "proposed 'a kind of all or nothing' choice" between fixed knowledge or meaning and "complete freeplay or undecidability."[10] The very idea of "freeplay," he suggested, was "Greatly overestimated in my texts in the United States" as a result of "inadequate translation" of the French term *jeu* ("play") used throughout "Structure, Sign, and Play."[11] Above all, he noted, by definition "no completeness is possible for undecidability."[12]

These attempts to parry his critics were to some extent doomed to fail, however. One of the fitting marks of Derrida's influence today is that his ideas are now so widely appropriated—not to mention mis- and re-appropriated—that they can no longer be returned to and fixed by their origins in his writing and thinking.

NOTES

1   Anonymous, "Most Cited Authors in the Humanities, 2007," *Times Higher Education*, 28 April 2009, accessed March 2, 2018, https://www.timeshighereducation.com/news/most-cited-authors-of-books-in-the-humanities-2007/405956.article?storyCode=405956&sectioncode=26.

2   Sarah Wood, *Derrida's Writing and Difference: A Reader's Guide* (London: Continuum, 2009), 169.

3   Judith Butler, *Gender Trouble: Feminism and the Subversion of Identity* (London: Routledge, 1999), x.

4   Butler, *Gender Trouble*, 54 and n.6.

5   Judith Butler, "Jacques Derrida," *London Review of Books*, Vol. 26, no. 21, November 4, 2004, 32.

6   Jacques Derrida, Gayatri Chakravorty Spivak, and Judith P. Butler, *Of Grammatology* (40th anniversary edition) (Baltimore: The Johns Hopkins University Press, 2016).

7   Raymond Tallis, *Not Saussure: A Critique of Post-Saussurean Literary Theory* (London: Macmillan Press, 1988).

8   Barry Smith *et al*, "Letter," *The Times* (London). Saturday, May 9, 1992.

9   Kurt Andersen, "How America Lost Its Mind," *The Atlantic Monthly*, September 2017, accessed March 2, 2018, https://www.theatlantic.com/magazine/archive/2017/09/how-america-lost-its-mind/534231/.

10 Jacques Derrida, *Limited Inc*, trans Samuel Weber (Evanston IL: Northwestern University Press, 1988), 115.

11 Derrida, *Limited Inc*, 115–16.

12 Derrida, *Limited Inc*, 116.

MODULE 12
WHERE NEXT?

KEY POINTS

- "Structure, Sign and Play" looks set to retain its key place in understanding Derrida's work and poststructuralism more broadly.

- The insights of "Structure, Sign and Play" continue to provide a means of critiquing and seeing through fixed ideas of knowledge and meaning.

- "Structure, Sign and Play" has a seminal status in intellectual history as the first text of poststructuralism.

Potential

The classic status of Jacques Derrida's "Structure, Sign, and Play in the Discourse of the Human Sciences" is hardly in doubt. Its place in the canon of literary theory is ensured by its pivotal role as the hinge between two of the major intellectual movements of the twentieth century: structuralism and poststructuralism. Along with the works Derrida published the following year, the 1966 essay helped usher in a radical reconsideration of the relationship between language and knowledge across the human sciences. It is through this seminal moment of opening up the humanities and social sciences to a radical notion of play and to the notion of deconstruction that "Structure, Sign and Play" continues to be read and to inspire new work.

At the same time, however, despite its privileged place in the history of literary theory, "Structure, Sign and Play" is only one element in the vast oeuvre that Derrida produced over the course of his academic career. The ideas and terminology put forward in it had already appeared in Derrida's earlier writings, and were to be

> **66** ... to put it playfully and with a certain immodesty, one has not yet begun to read me ... even though there are, to be sure, many very good readers. **99**
>
> Jacques Derrida, *Learning to Live Finally: The Last Interview*

considerably elaborated and extrapolated from over the next five decades. Because of that, and in fittingly Derridean style, "Structure, Sign and Play" seems often to disappear as an "origin" or "center" for his ideas, turning ceaselessly into all its subsequent reiterations.

Future Directions

Derrida continues to stimulate new work across the humanities and social sciences today. Since 2008, Edinburgh University Press has printed a biannual journal dedicated to his work, *Derrida Today*, reaffirming his persistent status as one of the most—if not *the* most—important philosophers of the late twentieth century. The journal's contents are a testament to the continuing fecundity of Derrida's work and to the wide array of philosophical and political arenas in which it has sown the seeds of new inquiry. Among the topics analyzed in 2017 alone were deconstruction and humanitarian aid,[1] deconstruction and the notion of political sovereignty,[2] and Derrida and the imagination of ghosts "On the Run."[3]

Given the richness of the work Derrida produced after and around "Structure, Sign, and Play," it is difficult to predict the future directions in which scholars will take his work. Though Benoît Dillet, Iain MacKenzie, and Robert Porter have written of poststructuralism as being "submerged" or "tamed" in modern scholarship, it is clear that it remains a potent force in academia.[4] Perhaps nowhere is this clearer than in the work of Judith Butler, who, since 1990's *Gender Trouble* has produced a wide-ranging corpus of philosophically and politically radical works, which turn the insights of "Structure, Sign and Play" and Derrida's other works towards significant political questions including ethics, segregation, and hate speech.[5]

Summary

"Structure, Sign and Play" is a crucial text for students in literature and the humanities for a number of reasons. As François Cusset (among many others) has noted, for historical reasons alone it must be classed as one of the most significant short texts of the late twentieth century.[6] As the "starting point" of poststructuralism it is a key text for anyone wishing to understand one of the dominant and radical movements in late twentieth century thought—the repercussions of which are still felt today. It is also a perfect point of entry into Derrida's own work. In a corpus filled with challenging texts, "Structure, Sign and Play" stands out as a remarkably self-contained, clear introduction to one of the most significant thinkers of our time.

Alongside the justified talk of both Derrida and the essay's particular significance, though, it is easy to neglect a simpler and equally important reason for reading "Structure, Sign, and Play." Though Derrida is a challenging writer, he is also a deeply stylish and "literary" philosopher. "Structure, Sign and Play" is an exemplary text from a philosopher known almost above all else for a writing style— elegant, complex, packed with puns and double readings—that tends to be at the center of the arguments between his defenders and his detractors. As noted above, Derrida's labeling as a literary theorist is, in some sense, a recognition that he is as literary as he is theoretical. And it is as much for this, as well as his seminal impact, that his work continues to be read today.

NOTES

1   Oliver Kelly, "Earthquakes: Deconstructing Humanitarianism," *Derrida Today*, Vol. 10, no. 1, May 2017: 38–50.

2   Paul Patton, "Deconstruction and the Problem of Sovereignty," *Derrida Today*, Vol. 10, no. 1, May 2017: 1–20.

3   Nicholas Royle, "On the Run," *Derrida Today*, Vol. 10, no. 2, Nov 2017: 125–41.

4   Benoît Dillet, Ian MacKenzie, and Robert Porter, ed., *The Edinburgh Companion to Poststructuralism* (Edinburgh: Edinburgh University Press, 2013), 507.

5   Kaye Mitchell, "Judith Butler" in *The Encyclopedia of Literary and Cultural Theory*, eds. Gregory Castle, Robert Eaglestone, and M. Keith Booker (Chichester: Wiley-Blackwell, 2011), 514–20.

6   François Cusset, *French Theory: How Foucault, Derrida, Deleuze, & Co. Transformed the Intellectual Life of the United States*, trans. Jeff Fort (Minneapolis: University of Minnesota Press, 2008), 31.

GLOSSARY

GLOSSARY OF TERMS

Analytical philosophy: the main style of academic philosophy taught and researched in Anglo-American universities; with an emphasis on formal logic and linguistic clarity it is often considered to be in opposition to the more literary approaches associated with continental philosophy.

Anti-rationalism: often used in the derogatory sense, to describe points of view that challenge the dominant paradigms of reason and logic in Western thought.

Bricolage: literally meaning "DIY" or "tinkering" in French that, via the work of Claude Lévi-Strauss and Gerard Genette, became current as a term for using multiple methodologies or materials simultaneously in anthropology and literary theory.

Colonialism: the policies of nations that annex or extend authority over other nations in order to maintain an empire and use the resources of those nations for the benefit of the colonizing power. It is particularly associated with the expansionist efforts of European nations from the fifteenth to the mid-twentieth century, including France and Great Britain.

Contingency: in philosophy, the status of propositions or situations that are not intrinsically necessary or true in all contexts, but which depend on other propositions or situations for their truth or existence. In structural linguistics a word's meaning, for instance, is contingent upon its place in the overall structure of a language.

Deconstruction: a term drawn from the work of French philosopher Jacques Derrida for an interpretative mode that seeks to reveal the internal contradictions and fault lines of texts by focusing on the instability of language and the impossibility of fixing meaning; it is particularly associated with poststructuralism.

Destruktion: a German word, "destruktion" is only used in philosophy and does not have the nihilistic overtones that "destruction" has in French or in English.

Différance: a term coined by Jacques Derrida meaning simultaneously "difference of meaning" and "deferral of meaning." Différance refers to the idea, fundamental in Derrida's work, that because all meaning arises from difference between terms, meaning is always in the process of being made and can never be said to have finally arrived. Meaning therefore is generated through *difference* and is always *deferred*.

École Normale Supérieure (ENS): a so-called *grande école* in Paris, the ENS is arguably the most prestigious higher-education institution in France. Founded in 1794 to train teachers, it is highly selective and is the *alma mater* of an astonishing percentage of France's most famous intellectuals and politicians.

Episteme: the dominant structure of knowledge in a given era or paradigm, deriving from the ancient Greek for knowledge or understanding; used by Jacques Derrida and Michel Foucault, among others.

Eschatology: literally the study of "last things" or the end of the world; taken from theology.

Freeplay: the unfixed status of meanings and interpretations within the shifting structures that create meaning in the world. From Jacques

Derrida's use of the French word *jeu*—literally "play" or "game"—in his essay "Structure, Sign, and Play in the Discourse of the Human Sciences."

French Theory: the body of work produced by influential thinkers in structuralism and poststructuralism during the 1960s and 1970s. A catch-all term often employed by historians of late twentieth-century thought, though there is no defined corpus or single outlook associated with French Theory. It is closely associated with the work of Michel Foucault and Jacques Derrida, among others.

Genetic structuralism: a branch of structuralist thought founded by Lucien Goldmann during the 1960s. It combines insights from both structuralism and Marxism to study the historic development of culture across time.

Human sciences: more generally in use in continental Europe to refer to the full range of subjects in the humanities and social sciences, including, but not limited to, literary studies, anthropology, sociology, and philosophy.

Johns Hopkins University: an American university founded in 1876 in Baltimore, Maryland. It is noted as one of the world's top educational institutions.

Linguistics: the scientific study of language.

Logocentrism: the notion that speech expresses external and fundamental reality, and does so more purely than writing. Derrida carried out a deep critique of logocentric ideas across his work, particularly in *Of Grammatology*.

Lycée Louis-le-Grand: a public secondary school in Paris. One of France's most prestigious schools it is known above all for its *classes préparatoires*, designed to prepare students who have already graduated from secondary education for entrance to France's most competitive public universities, the so-called *grandes écoles*.

Marxism: a broad political, intellectual and philosophical school based around the theories of the German philosopher, economist, and revolutionary socialist Karl Marx. Associated with Communism, Marxism provides a range of ways for analyzing the relations between culture, society, and economics.

Meta-language: a language used to describe or make statements about another language.

Mimesis: from the ancient Greek word meaning literally "imitation" or "mimicking," mimesis was popularized in the mid-twentieth century by the literary critic Erich Auerbach's study *Mimesis:The Representation of Reality in Western Literature* (1946). For René Girard, in studies including *Things Hidden Since the Foundation of the World* (1978) it became a fundamental element of human culture and consciousness, structuring desire, violence, and the anthropology of religion.

Nihilism: philosophical stances that maintain certain aspects of life generally held to be meaningful—from morality to ethics—are in fact meaningless or lack intrinsic value. Often employed pejoratively.

Nouvelle critique: a type of structuralist literary criticism in France during the 1950s and 1960s, particularly the work of Roland Barthes.

Play: see Freeplay.

Poststructuralism: a philosophical or theoretic school generally held to have been founded by Jacques Derrida. Poststructuralism grew out of structuralism, but was opposed to that school's determinism and proposed instead a radically open-ended approach to meaning and interpretation.

Pseudophilosophy: a pejorative term for works purporting to be philosophy, but which are considered by their critics to have no philosophical value.

Relativism: the philosophical stance that truths and knowledge are not intrinsically fixed, but are only true in relation to specific contexts or differences in the perception of individuals. Like nihilism it is often used in a pejorative sense.

Semiology: deriving from the Ancient Greek *semeion*, "sign," and also referred to as "semiotics," it is the study of signs, symbols, and their use or interpretation. While "semiotics" has a long history, "semiology," with specific reference to the human sciences, was first suggested by Ferdinand de Saussure in his 1916 *Course in General Linguistics*.

Sign: used in its technical sense by the linguist Ferdinand de Saussure, the sign is the basic unit of language, consisting of both the "signifier" (a word or sound) and the "signified" (the concept linked to that word/sound within the overall structure of the language).

Signified: used in its technical sense by the linguist Ferdinand de Saussure, the signified is the concept or "real world object" linked to a given word ("signifier") within a given language.

Signifier: used in its technical sense by the linguist Ferdinand de Saussure, the signifier is a word or sound pattern that carries a given meaning (the "signified") within a language.

Sokal Hoax: a famous academic prank carried out by the physicist Alan Sokal in 1996. Sokal concocted an elaborate parody of poststructuralist writing in an article that purported to give a poststructuralist account of gravity. The article "Towards a Transformative Hermeneutics of Quantum Gravity" was published in the well-known theoretical journal *Social Text*, leading Sokal to suggest that much poststructuralist philosophy and analysis lacked intellectual rigor and worth.

Structuralism: a methodology or theoretical stance drawn originally from structural linguistics as elaborated by Ferdinand de Saussure. Broadly, structuralism seeks to uncover the structures that lie underneath elements of human culture and define how those elements become intelligible to other humans. It is particularly associated with the influential theorists of 1950s and 1960s France, including Claude Lévi-Strauss and Roland Barthes.

Structural anthropology: a school of anthropology that draws on the influential work of French anthropologist Claude Lévi-Strauss. It uses insights taken from the work of structural linguist Ferdinand de Saussure to examine the deep mental structures that, Lévi-Strauss suggested, underlie and inform all cultures.

Subaltern: first used by the Italian Marxist theorist Antonio Gramsci to denote colonial populations that are excluded, socially, geographically, and politically, from the power structures of colonizing powers, the term has been at the center of work by the theorist Gayatri Spivak since the late 1970s.

Teleology: a theological and philosophical term for explanations of phenomena that seek to relate them to a supposed final purpose or goal.

Vichy France: the regime nominally governing France from 1940–1944, during World War II. Though the country was in fact under the control of Nazi Germany, the Vichy regime, headed by Phillipe Pétain, supposedly governed the country and many of its colonial possessions overseas. Authoritarian and conservative, the Vichy government's reactionary policies included the implementation of anti-Semitic laws.

Yale School: a loose group of influential literary critics and theorists affiliated with Yale University from the 1970s through to the 1990s, including Paul de Man, J. Hillis Miller, and Jacques Derrida. The Yale School is particularly associated with deconstruction.

PEOPLE MENTIONED IN THE TEXT

Woody Allen (b. 1935) is an American filmmaker, actor and comedian. He has made over 50 films, including the 1997 *Deconstructing Harry*, the title of which references Derridean deconstruction.

Derek Attridge (b. 1945) is a South African-born British literary critic and theorist, specializing in modernist literature and literary theory. He is best known for his study *Peculiar Language: Literature as Difference from the Renaissance to James Joyce*.

Roland Barthes (1915–80) was an influential French literary theorist, critic, linguist, and semiotician particularly active during 1950s and 1960s. Renowned for his controversial stances on traditional critical approaches, including his famous "Death of the Author" thesis (1968), Barthes' works also include, *Writing, Degree Zero* (1953), *Mythologies* (1957), and *S/Z* (1970).

Alan Bass is a translator and psychoanalyst based in New York. He is best known for his translations of Jacques Derrida's *Writing and Difference* (1979), *Positions* (1982), *Margins: Of Philosophy* (1984), and *The Post Card* (1987).

Walter Jackson Bate (1918–99) was an American literary critic and biographer. He is best known for his biographies *John Keats* (1963) and *Samuel Johnson* (1977), as well as his study *The Burden of the Past and the English Poet* (1970).

Geoffrey Bennington (b. 1956) is a literary critic and philosopher best known for his work on and with Jacques Derrida, including the collaborative text *Jacques Derrida* (1991). He is currently the Asa Griggs Candler Professor of French and Professor of Comparative Literature at Emory University, Atlanta, Georgia.

Pierre Bourdieu (1930–2002) was a French sociologist and anthropologist strongly influenced by structuralism and the work of Claude Lévi-Strauss. He is best known for his book *Distinction: A Social Critique of the Judgement of Taste* (1979).

Judith Butler (b. 1956) is an American philosopher and theorist known for her groundbreaking work on gender and sexuality in books that include *Gender Trouble: Feminism and the Subversion of Identity* (1990). She is currently Maxine Elliot Professor of Comparative Literature and Critical Theory at the University of California, Berkeley.

Jonathan Culler (b. 1944) is a literary critic and theorist based at Cornell University, New York. He is best known for his work on structuralism and deconstruction in studies that include *Structuralist Poetics: Structuralism, Linguistics and the Study of Literature* (1977) and *On Deconstruction: Theory and Criticism after Structuralism* (1983).

François Cusset (b. 1969) is a French writer and intellectual historian who teaches at the University of Naterre, France. He is best known for his 2003 study *French Theory: How Foucault, Derrida, Deleuze, & Co Transformed the Intellectual Life of the United States*.

Eugenio Donato (1937–83) was an Armenian-Italian literary critic and theorist known for his work on structuralism and poststructuralism in the United States. He is best known for organizing the 1966 structuralist conference "The Languages of Criticism and the Sciences of Man" with Richard Macksey and co-editing its proceedings, *The Structuralist Controversy: The Languages of Criticism* and *The Science of Man* (1972).

François Dosse (b. 1950) is a French historian specializing in intellectual history. He is best known for his work on French literary theory and philosophy of the 1960s, including his two-volume *History of Structuralism* (1991–1992).

Michel Foucault (1926–84) was a French historian and philosopher known for his work on power, knowledge, and sexuality. His major works include *The Order of Things* (1996) and his three-volume *History of Sexuality* (1976–1984).

Sigmund Freud (1856–1939) was an Austrian neurologist famous as the founder of psychoanalysis, one of the major medical and intellectual movements of the twentieth century. Though many of his theories have been discredited, his work remains a formative influence in many areas of intellectual life, including literary theory. Major works include *The Interpretation of Dreams* (1900) and *Civilization and its Discontents* (1930).

Gerard Genette (b. 1930) is a French critic and literary theorist best known for his contributions to the structuralist movement. His major works include *Palimpsests: Literature in the Second Degree* (1982) and *Paratexts. Thresholds of Interpretation* (1997).

René Girard (1923–2015) was a French historian and philosopher known for his "mimetic" theory, and his work on anthropology and the history of religion. Among his major texts are *Violence and the Sacred* (1972) and *Things Hidden Since the Foundation of the World* (1987).

Lucien Goldmann (1913–70) was a French philosopher, Marxist theorist and sociologist originally from Romania. A key figure in the structuralist school, Goldmann was also one of its most prominent critics. His major works include *Towards a Sociology of the Novel* (1964).

Martin Heidegger (1889–1976) was an influential German philosopher known for his work on hermeneutics, ontology, and time. A primary influence on Jacques Derrida, Heidegger's major works include *Being and Time* (1927), Heidegger is also regarded as a major influence on both structuralism and poststructuralism in general.

Jacques Lacan (1901–81) was a French psychoanalyst and philosopher whose work was highly influential in 1960s and 70s French thought. He is best known for his *Écrits* (1966).

Claude Lévi-Strauss (1908–2009) was an influential French anthropologist credited with founding structural anthropology and exerting a formative influence on structuralism in post-war France. His major works include *Tristes Tropiques* (1955), *Structural Anthropology* (1958), and *The Savage Mind* (1962).

Richard Macksey (b. 1931) is a literary critic and theorist based at Johns Hopkins University, Baltimore. He is best known for organizing, with Eugenio Donato, the 1966 structuralist conference "The Languages of Criticism and the Sciences of Man" and co-editing its proceedings, *The Structuralist Controversy: The Languages of Criticism* and *The Science of Man* (1972).

Paul de Man (1919–83) was a Belgian-born literary critic and theorist known for his work on deconstruction and his central role in forming the so-called Yale School of literary criticism. A close friend of Jacques Derrida, his major works include *Allegories of Reading* (1979) and *Blindness and Insight* (1983).

Marcel Mauss (1872–1950) was an influential French sociologist and anthropologist. A significant influence on the structural anthropologist Claude Lévi-Strauss, Mauss is best known today for his 1925 study *The Gift*.

J. Hillis Miller (b. 1928) is an American literary critic and theorist known for his work on deconstruction and his role in forming the so-called Yale School of literary criticism. His major texts include *The Linguistic Moment* (1985) and *The Ethics of Reading* (1987).

Michel de Montaigne (1533–92) was one of the most important and lastingly influential writers and philosophers of the sixteenth century. He is known above all for the three books of *The Essays*, first published in 1580.

Friedrich Nietzsche (1844–1900) was one of the most influential German writers of the nineteenth century. A philosopher and classical scholar he was known for his literary style and radical questioning of received values. Among his best-known works are *On Truth and Lies in a Nonmoral Sense* (1873) and *On the Genealogy of Morality* (1887). He is regarded as a major influence on both Jacques Derrida and poststructuralist thought more generally.

Oedipus was the mythical king of the ancient Greek city of Thebes whose story is the plot of Sophocles' tragedy *Oedipus Tyrannus*. The exemplary figure of the tragic hero, Oedipus unwittingly killed his own father and married his mother, acts that later brought a plague on his kingdom. When he sought out the cause of the plague from the blind soothsayer Tiresias, and discovered his own acts, he plucked out his own eyes and went into exile.

Jean-Jacques Rousseau (1712–78) was a Swiss-born philosopher and writer whose work was influential during the Enlightenment and after. A constant touchstone for Jacques Derrida, he is best known now for his novel *Emile, or On Education* (1762) and his autobiographical *Confessions* (published posthumously in 1782).

Ferdinand de Saussure (1857–1913) was a Swiss linguist and semiotician whose works were vastly influential on linguistics, laying the foundations of both structural linguistics and structuralism more generally. He is best known for the posthumously published *Course in General Linguistics* (1916).

John Searle (b. 1932) is an American philosopher; currently the Willis S. and Marion Slusser Professor Emeritus of the Philosophy of Mind and Language at the University of California, Berkeley, he is known for his contributions to the philosophy of language and philosophy of mind; he remains best known for his early book *Speech Acts: An Essay in the Philosophy of Language* (1969).

Barry Smith (b. 1952) is a British-born philosopher teaching at the University of Buffalo, New York. A specialist in German philosophy, he is well known for spearheading the campaign to prevent Jacques Derrida from being offered an honorary doctorate by the University of Cambridge in 1992.

Alan Sokal (b. 1955) is a physicist and mathematician known as a critic of postmodernism and poststructuralism in the wake of his widely publicized hoaxing of the theory in the journal *Social Text* in

1996. He is best known for his book *Fashionable Nonsense: Postmodern Intellectuals' Abuse of Science* (1997), co-authored with Jean Bricmont.

Gayatri Chakravorty Spivak (b. 1942) is a literary theorist and feminist widely seen as the mother of postcolonial studies. University Professor at Columbia University, she is best known for her 1983 essay "Can the Subaltern Speak?" and for her translation and preface to Jacques Derrida's *Of Grammatology*.

Raymond Tallis (b. 1946) is British doctor, philosopher, and critic. Alongside his medical work he is known for a number of philosophical books on the human mind and experience. A well-known critic of poststructuralism, his best known literary-theoretical works are *Not Saussure* (1988) and *Theorrhoea and After* (1998).

Tiresias is a mythological character, a blind soothsayer from the ancient Greek city of Thebes. He is known from a number of myths, including the story of Oedipus, where the facts revealed by his prophecy lead to the tragic outcome of Oedipus's tale.

WORKS CITED

WORKS CITED

Andersen, Kurt Andersen. "How America Lost Its Mind." *The Atlantic Monthly*, September 2017. Accessed March 2, 2018. https://www.theatlantic.com/magazine/archive/2017/09/how-america-lost-its-mind/534231/

Anonymous. "Most cited authors in the humanities, 2007." *Times Higher Education*, April 28, 2009. Accessed March 2, 2018. https://www.timeshighereducation.com/news/most-cited-authors-in-the-humanities-2007/405956.article?storyCode=405956&sectioncode=26

Anonymous. "Obituary: Jacques Derrida." *The Economist*, October 21, 2004.

Attridge, Derek, and Thomas Baldwin. "Obituary: Jacques Derrida." *The Guardian*, October 11, 2004. Accessed March 2, 2018. https://www.theguardian.com/news/2004/oct/11/guardianobituaries.france

Baring, Edward. *Young Derrida and French Philosophy, 1945–1968*. Cambridge: Cambridge University Press, 2011.

Bennington, Geoffrey, "Embarrassing Ourselves." *Los Angeles Review of Books*, March 20, 2016. Accessed March 2, 2018. https://lareviewofbooks.org/article/embarrassing-ourselves/#

Bennington, Geoffrey, and Jacques Derrida. *Jacques Derrida*. Translated by Geoffrey Bennington. Chicago: University of Chicago Press, 1999.

Butler, Judith. *Gender Trouble: Feminism and the Subversion of Identity*. London: Routledge, 1999.

- "Jacques Derrida." *London Review of Books*, Vol. 26, no. 21, November 4, 2004, 32.

Coker, John. "Jacques Derrida." In *The Blackwell Guide to Continental Philosophy*, edited by Robert Solomon and David Sherman, 265–284. Oxford: Blackwell, 2003.

Culler, Jonathan. *On Deconstruction: Theory and Criticism after Structuralism*. Ithaca NY: Cornell University Press, 1983.

Cusset, François. *French Theory: How Foucault, Derrida, Deleuze, & Co. Transformed the Intellectual Life of the United States*. Translated by Jeff Fort. Minneapolis: University of Minnesota Press, 2008.

Derrida, Jacques. *La Voix et le Phénomène: Introduction au problème du signe dans la phénoménologie de Husserl*. Paris: Presses Universitaires de France, 1967.

- *De la grammatologie*. Paris: Minuit, 1967.

- *L'écriture et la différence*. Paris: Seuil, 1967.

- "The Ends of Man." *Philosophy and Phenomenological Research* 30, 1 (1969): 31–57.

- *Speech and Phenomena and Other Essays on Husserl's Theory of Signs*. Translated by David B. Allison, Newton Garver. Evanston: Northwestern University Press, 1973.

- *Limited Inc*. Translated by Samuel Weber. Evanston IL: Northwestern University Press, 1988.

- *Of Grammatology* (Corrected Edition). Translated by Gayatri Chakravorty Spivak. Baltimore: Johns Hopkins University Press, 1998.

- *Writing and Difference*. Translated by Alan Bass. London: Routledge, 2001.

- "Structure, Sign and Play in the Discourse of the Human Sciences." In *Writing and Difference*, 351–70. Translated by Alan Bass. London: Routledge, 2001.

- "Letter to a Japanese friend." In *Psyche: Inventions of the Other,* vol. 2, edited by Peggy Kamuf and Elizabeth Rottenberg. Stanford: Stanford University Press, 2007.

- "Sokal et Bricmont ne sont pas sérieux." *Le Monde*, November 20, 1997, 17.

- *Monolingualism of the Other; or, The Prosthesis of Origin*. Translated by Patrick Mensah. Stanford: Stanford University Press, 1998.

Derrida, Jacques, G. Scarpetta, and J. L. Houdebine. "Interview: Jacques Derrida." *Diacritics* 2, no. 4. (1972): 35–43.

Derrida, Jacques, and J.-L. Houdebine. "Interview: Jacques Derrida." *Diacritics* 3, no. 1. (1973): 33–46.

Derrida, Jacques, and Maurizio Ferrari. *A Taste for the Secret*. Translated by Giacomo Donis, edited by Giacomo Donis and David Webb. London: Polity, 2001.

Derrida, Jacques, Gayatri Chakravorty Spivak, and Judith P. Butler. *Of Grammatology*. Translated by Gayatri Chakravorty Spivak. Baltimore: The Johns Hopkins University Press, 2016.

Dillet, Benoît, Ian MacKenzie, and Robert Porter ed. *The Edinburgh Companion to Poststructuralism*. Edinburgh: Edinburgh University Press, 2013.

Dosse, François. *History of Structuralism, Volume I: The Rising Sign, 1945–1966*. Translated by Deborah Glassman. Minneapolis: University of Minnesota Press, 1997.

Gelley, Alexander. "Form as Force." *Diacritics* 2, no. 1. 1972): 9–13

Genette, Gerard. *Figures I*. Paris: Éditions du Seuil, 1966.

Girard, René. "Tiresias and the Critic." In *The Structuralist Controversy: The Languages of Criticism and the Sciences of Man*, edited by Richard Macksey and Eugenio Donato, 15–20. Baltimore: Johns Hopkins University Press, 1972.

Goldmann, Lucien. "Structure: Human Reality and Methodological Concept." In *The Structuralist Controversy: The Languages of Criticism and the Sciences of Man*, edited by Richard Macksey and Eugenio Donato, 98–110. Baltimore: Johns Hopkins University Press, 1972.

Hill, Leslie. *The Cambridge Introduction to Jacques Derrida*. Cambridge: Cambridge University Press, 2007.

Hsu, Joanne A. "Saussure." In *The Encyclopedia of Literary and Cultural Theory*, edited by Gregory Castle, Robert Eaglestone, and M. Keith Booker. Chichester: Wiley-Blackwell, 2011.

Kandell, Jonathan. "Jacques Derrida, Abstruse Theorist, Dies at 74." *The New York Times*, October 10, 2004.

Kelly, Oliver. "Earthquakes: Deconstructing Humanitarianism." *Derrida Today*, Vol.10, no. 1 (May 2017): 38–50.

Klein, Richard. "Prolegomenon to Derrida." *Diacritics* 2, no. 4. (1972): 29–34.

Lacan, Jacques. "Of Structure as an Inmixing of an Otherness Prerequisite to Any Subject Whatever." In *The Structuralist Controversy: The Languages of Criticism and the Sciences of Man*, edited by Richard Macksey and Eugenio Donato, 186–195. Baltimore: Johns Hopkins University Press, 1972.

Lévi-Strauss, Claude. *La Pensée sauvage*. Paris: Plon, 1962.

- *The Savage Mind*. Translated by Anonymous. London: Weidenfeld and Nicolson, 1966.

Lucy, Niall. *A Derrida Dictionary*. Oxford: Blackwell, 2004.

Macksey, Richard, and Eugenio Donato, ed. *The Structuralist Controversy: The Languages of Criticism and the Sciences of Man*. Baltimore: Johns Hopkins University Press, 1972.

de Man, Paul. *The Resistance to Theory*. Minneapolis: University of Minnesota Press, 1986.

Miller, J. Hillis. "Derrida and de Man: Two Rhetorics of Deconstruction." In *A Companion to Derrida,* edited by Zeynep Direk and Leonard Lawlor. Oxford: Blackwell, 2014.

Mitchell, Kaye. "Judith Butler." In *The Encyclopedia of Literary and Cultural Theory*, edited by Gregory Castle, Robert Eaglestone, and M. Keith Booker, 514–520. Chichester: Wiley-Blackwell, 2011.

Patton, Paul. "Deconstruction and the Problem of Sovereignty." *Derrida Today*, Vol. 10, no. 1 (May 2017): 1–20.

Peeters, Benoît. *Derrida: A Biography*. Translated by Andrew Brown. London: Polity, 2013.

Royle, Nicholas. "On the Run," *Derrida Today*, Vol. 10, no. 2 (Nov 2017): 125–41.

Saint-Jacques, Denis. "Jacques Derrida, *La Voix et le Phénomène*, Paris, P.U.F., Collection «Épiméthée», 1967; *L'Écriture et la différence*, Paris, Seuil, Collection «Tel Quel», 1967; *De la grammatologie*, Éditions de Minuit, Collection «Critique», 1967;" *Études littéraires* 1, no. 3 (1968): 452–55.

Saussure, Ferdinand de. *Course in General Linguistics*, edited by Charles Bally and Albert Sechehaye, translated by Wade Baskin. New York: The Philosophical Library, 1959.

Searle, John R. "The Word Turned Upside Down." *The New York Review of Books*, October 27, 1983. Accessed March 2, 2018. http://www.nybooks.com/articles/archives/1983/oct/27/the-word-turned-upside-down/

Smith, Barry *et al*. "Letter." *The Times*, London. Saturday, May 9, 1992.

Smith, Barry, and Jeffrey Sims. "Revisiting the Derrida Affair with Barry Smith." *Sophia* Vol. 38, no 2 (September–October 1999): 142–70.

Sokal, Alan. "Transgressing the Boundaries: Towards a Transformative Hermeneutics of Quantum Gravity." *Social Text*, 46/47, (Spring/Summer. 1996): 217–52.

Sokal, Alan, and Jean Bricmont. *Fashionable Nonsense: Postmodern Intellectuals' Abuse of Science*. New York: Picador 1998.

Spivak, Gayatri Chakravorty. "Translator's Preface" in Jacques Derrida, *Of Grammatology*, translated by Gayatri Chakravorty Spivak. Baltimore: Johns Hopkins University Press, 1997.

- *A Critique of Postcolonial Reason: Toward a History of the Vanishing Present*. Cambridge MA: Harvard University Press, 1999.

Tallis, Raymond. *Not Saussure. A Critique of Post-Saussurean Literary Theory.* London: Macmillan Press, 1988.

Wood, Sarah. *Derrida's Writing and Difference: A Reader's Guide*. London: Continuum, 2009.

THE MACAT LIBRARY
BY DISCIPLINE

AFRICANA STUDIES

Chinua Achebe's *An Image of Africa: Racism in Conrad's Heart of Darkness*
W. E. B. Du Bois's *The Souls of Black Folk*
Zora Neale Huston's *Characteristics of Negro Expression*
Martin Luther King Jr's *Why We Can't Wait*
Toni Morrison's *Playing in the Dark: Whiteness in the American Literary Imagination*

ANTHROPOLOGY

Arjun Appadurai's *Modernity at Large: Cultural Dimensions of Globalisation*
Philippe Ariès's *Centuries of Childhood*
Franz Boas's *Race, Language and Culture*
Kim Chan & Renée Mauborgne's *Blue Ocean Strategy*
Jared Diamond's *Guns, Germs & Steel: the Fate of Human Societies*
Jared Diamond's *Collapse: How Societies Choose to Fail or Survive*
E. E. Evans-Pritchard's *Witchcraft, Oracles and Magic Among the Azande*
James Ferguson's *The Anti-Politics Machine*
Clifford Geertz's *The Interpretation of Cultures*
David Graeber's *Debt: the First 5000 Years*
Karen Ho's *Liquidated: An Ethnography of Wall Street*
Geert Hofstede's *Culture's Consequences: Comparing Values, Behaviors, Institutes and Organizations across Nations*
Claude Lévi-Strauss's *Structural Anthropology*
Jay Macleod's *Ain't No Makin' It: Aspirations and Attainment in a Low-Income Neighborhood*
Saba Mahmood's *The Politics of Piety: The Islamic Revival and the Feminist Subject*
Marcel Mauss's *The Gift*

BUSINESS

Jean Lave & Etienne Wenger's *Situated Learning*
Theodore Levitt's *Marketing Myopia*
Burton G. Malkiel's *A Random Walk Down Wall Street*
Douglas McGregor's *The Human Side of Enterprise*
Michael Porter's *Competitive Strategy: Creating and Sustaining Superior Performance*
John Kotter's *Leading Change*
C. K. Prahalad & Gary Hamel's *The Core Competence of the Corporation*

CRIMINOLOGY

Michelle Alexander's *The New Jim Crow: Mass Incarceration in the Age of Colorblindness*
Michael R. Gottfredson & Travis Hirschi's *A General Theory of Crime*
Richard Herrnstein & Charles A. Murray's *The Bell Curve: Intelligence and Class Structure in American Life*
Elizabeth Loftus's *Eyewitness Testimony*
Jay Macleod's *Ain't No Makin' It: Aspirations and Attainment in a Low-Income Neighborhood*
Philip Zimbardo's *The Lucifer Effect*

ECONOMICS

Janet Abu-Lughod's *Before European Hegemony*
Ha-Joon Chang's *Kicking Away the Ladder*
David Brion Davis's *The Problem of Slavery in the Age of Revolution*
Milton Friedman's *The Role of Monetary Policy*
Milton Friedman's *Capitalism and Freedom*
David Graeber's *Debt: the First 5000 Years*
Friedrich Hayek's *The Road to Serfdom*
Karen Ho's *Liquidated: An Ethnography of Wall Street*

The Macat Library By Discipline

John Maynard Keynes's *The General Theory of Employment, Interest and Money*
Charles P. Kindleberger's *Manias, Panics and Crashes*
Robert Lucas's *Why Doesn't Capital Flow from Rich to Poor Countries?*
Burton G. Malkiel's *A Random Walk Down Wall Street*
Thomas Robert Malthus's *An Essay on the Principle of Population*
Karl Marx's *Capital*
Thomas Piketty's *Capital in the Twenty-First Century*
Amartya Sen's *Development as Freedom*
Adam Smith's *The Wealth of Nations*
Nassim Nicholas Taleb's *The Black Swan: The Impact of the Highly Improbable*
Amos Tversky's & Daniel Kahneman's *Judgment under Uncertainty: Heuristics and Biases*
Mahbub Ul Haq's *Reflections on Human Development*
Max Weber's *The Protestant Ethic and the Spirit of Capitalism*

FEMINISM AND GENDER STUDIES

Judith Butler's *Gender Trouble*
Simone De Beauvoir's *The Second Sex*
Michel Foucault's *History of Sexuality*
Betty Friedan's *The Feminine Mystique*
Saba Mahmood's *The Politics of Piety: The Islamic Revival and the Feminist Subjec*t
Joan Wallach Scott's *Gender and the Politics of History*
Mary Wollstonecraft's *A Vindication of the Rights of Woman*
Virginia Woolf's *A Room of One's Own*

GEOGRAPHY

The Brundtland Report's *Our Common Future*
Rachel Carson's *Silent Spring*
Charles Darwin's *On the Origin of Species*
James Ferguson's *The Anti-Politics Machine*
Jane Jacobs's *The Death and Life of Great American Cities*
James Lovelock's *Gaia: A New Look at Life on Earth*
Amartya Sen's *Development as Freedom*
Mathis Wackernagel & William Rees's *Our Ecological Footprint*

HISTORY

Janet Abu-Lughod's *Before European Hegemony*
Benedict Anderson's *Imagined Communities*
Bernard Bailyn's *The Ideological Origins of the American Revolution*
Hanna Batatu's *The Old Social Classes And The Revolutionary Movements Of Iraq*
Christopher Browning's *Ordinary Men: Reserve Police Batallion 101 and the Final Solution in Poland*
Edmund Burke's *Reflections on the Revolution in France*
William Cronon's *Nature's Metropolis: Chicago And The Great West*
Alfred W. Crosby's *The Columbian Exchange*
Hamid Dabashi's *Iran: A People Interrupted*
David Brion Davis's *The Problem of Slavery in the Age of Revolution*
Nathalie Zemon Davis's *The Return of Martin Guerre*
Jared Diamond's *Guns, Germs & Steel: the Fate of Human Societies*
Frank Dikotter's *Mao's Great Famine*
John W Dower's *War Without Mercy: Race And Power In The Pacific War*
W. E. B. Du Bois's *The Souls of Black Folk*
Richard J. Evans's *In Defence of History*
Lucien Febvre's *The Problem of Unbelief in the 16th Century*
Sheila Fitzpatrick's *Everyday Stalinism*

Eric Foner's *Reconstruction: America's Unfinished Revolution, 1863-1877*
Michel Foucault's *Discipline and Punish*
Michel Foucault's *History of Sexuality*
Francis Fukuyama's *The End of History and the Last Man*
John Lewis Gaddis's *We Now Know: Rethinking Cold War History*
Ernest Gellner's *Nations and Nationalism*
Eugene Genovese's *Roll, Jordan, Roll: The World the Slaves Made*
Carlo Ginzburg's *The Night Battles*
Daniel Goldhagen's *Hitler's Willing Executioners*
Jack Goldstone's *Revolution and Rebellion in the Early Modern World*
Antonio Gramsci's *The Prison Notebooks*
Alexander Hamilton, John Jay & James Madison's *The Federalist Papers*
Christopher Hill's *The World Turned Upside Down*
Carole Hillenbrand's *The Crusades: Islamic Perspectives*
Thomas Hobbes's *Leviathan*
Eric Hobsbawm's *The Age Of Revolution*
John A. Hobson's *Imperialism: A Study*
Albert Hourani's *History of the Arab Peoples*
Samuel P. Huntington's *The Clash of Civilizations and the Remaking of World Order*
C. L. R. James's *The Black Jacobins*
Tony Judt's *Postwar: A History of Europe Since 1945*
Ernst Kantorowicz's *The King's Two Bodies: A Study in Medieval Political Theology*
Paul Kennedy's *The Rise and Fall of the Great Powers*
Ian Kershaw's *The "Hitler Myth": Image and Reality in the Third Reich*
John Maynard Keynes's *The General Theory of Employment, Interest and Money*
Charles P. Kindleberger's *Manias, Panics and Crashes*
Martin Luther King Jr's *Why We Can't Wait*
Henry Kissinger's *World Order: Reflections on the Character of Nations and the Course of History*
Thomas Kuhn's *The Structure of Scientific Revolutions*
Georges Lefebvre's *The Coming of the French Revolution*
John Locke's *Two Treatises of Government*
Niccolò Machiavelli's *The Prince*
Thomas Robert Malthus's *An Essay on the Principle of Population*
Mahmood Mamdani's *Citizen and Subject: Contemporary Africa And The Legacy Of Late Colonialism*
Karl Marx's *Capital*
Stanley Milgram's *Obedience to Authority*
John Stuart Mill's *On Liberty*
Thomas Paine's *Common Sense*
Thomas Paine's *Rights of Man*
Geoffrey Parker's *Global Crisis: War, Climate Change and Catastrophe in the Seventeenth Century*
Jonathan Riley-Smith's *The First Crusade and the Idea of Crusading*
Jean-Jacques Rousseau's *The Social Contract*
Joan Wallach Scott's *Gender and the Politics of History*
Theda Skocpol's *States and Social Revolutions*
Adam Smith's *The Wealth of Nations*
Timothy Snyder's *Bloodlands: Europe Between Hitler and Stalin*
Sun Tzu's *The Art of War*
Keith Thomas's *Religion and the Decline of Magic*
Thucydides's *The History of the Peloponnesian War*
Frederick Jackson Turner's *The Significance of the Frontier in American History*
Odd Arne Westad's *The Global Cold War: Third World Interventions And The Making Of Our Times*

The Macat Library By Discipline

LITERATURE

Chinua Achebe's *An Image of Africa: Racism in Conrad's Heart of Darkness*
Roland Barthes's *Mythologies*
Homi K. Bhabha's *The Location of Culture*
Judith Butler's *Gender Trouble*
Simone De Beauvoir's *The Second Sex*
Ferdinand De Saussure's *Course in General Linguistics*
T. S. Eliot's *The Sacred Wood: Essays on Poetry and Criticism*
Zora Neale Huston's *Characteristics of Negro Expression*
Toni Morrison's *Playing in the Dark: Whiteness in the American Literary Imagination*
Edward Said's *Orientalism*
Gayatri Chakravorty Spivak's *Can the Subaltern Speak?*
Mary Wollstonecraft's *A Vindication of the Rights of Women*
Virginia Woolf's *A Room of One's Own*

PHILOSOPHY

Elizabeth Anscombe's *Modern Moral Philosophy*
Hannah Arendt's *The Human Condition*
Aristotle's *Metaphysics*
Aristotle's *Nicomachean Ethics*
Edmund Gettier's *Is Justified True Belief Knowledge?*
Georg Wilhelm Friedrich Hegel's *Phenomenology of Spirit*
David Hume's *Dialogues Concerning Natural Religion*
David Hume's *The Enquiry for Human Understanding*
Immanuel Kant's *Religion within the Boundaries of Mere Reason*
Immanuel Kant's *Critique of Pure Reason*
Søren Kierkegaard's *The Sickness Unto Death*
Søren Kierkegaard's *Fear and Trembling*
C. S. Lewis's *The Abolition of Man*
Alasdair MacIntyre's *After Virtue*
Marcus Aurelius's *Meditations*
Friedrich Nietzsche's *On the Genealogy of Morality*
Friedrich Nietzsche's *Beyond Good and Evil*
Plato's *Republic*
Plato's *Symposium*
Jean-Jacques Rousseau's *The Social Contract*
Gilbert Ryle's *The Concept of Mind*
Baruch Spinoza's *Ethics*
Sun Tzu's *The Art of War*
Ludwig Wittgenstein's *Philosophical Investigations*

POLITICS

Benedict Anderson's *Imagined Communities*
Aristotle's *Politics*
Bernard Bailyn's *The Ideological Origins of the American Revolution*
Edmund Burke's *Reflections on the Revolution in France*
John C. Calhoun's *A Disquisition on Government*
Ha-Joon Chang's *Kicking Away the Ladder*
Hamid Dabashi's *Iran: A People Interrupted*
Hamid Dabashi's *Theology of Discontent: The Ideological Foundation of the Islamic Revolution in Iran*
Robert Dahl's *Democracy and its Critics*
Robert Dahl's *Who Governs?*
David Brion Davis's *The Problem of Slavery in the Age of Revolution*

Alexis De Tocqueville's *Democracy in America*
James Ferguson's *The Anti-Politics Machine*
Frank Dikotter's *Mao's Great Famine*
Sheila Fitzpatrick's *Everyday Stalinism*
Eric Foner's *Reconstruction: America's Unfinished Revolution, 1863-1877*
Milton Friedman's *Capitalism and Freedom*
Francis Fukuyama's *The End of History and the Last Man*
John Lewis Gaddis's *We Now Know: Rethinking Cold War History*
Ernest Gellner's *Nations and Nationalism*
David Graeber's *Debt: the First 5000 Years*
Antonio Gramsci's *The Prison Notebooks*
Alexander Hamilton, John Jay & James Madison's *The Federalist Papers*
Friedrich Hayek's *The Road to Serfdom*
Christopher Hill's *The World Turned Upside Down*
Thomas Hobbes's *Leviathan*
John A. Hobson's *Imperialism: A Study*
Samuel P. Huntington's *The Clash of Civilizations and the Remaking of World Order*
Tony Judt's *Postwar: A History of Europe Since 1945*
David C. Kang's *China Rising: Peace, Power and Order in East Asia*
Paul Kennedy's *The Rise and Fall of Great Powers*
Robert Keohane's *After Hegemony*
Martin Luther King Jr.'s *Why We Can't Wait*
Henry Kissinger's *World Order: Reflections on the Character of Nations and the Course of History*
John Locke's *Two Treatises of Government*
Niccolò Machiavelli's *The Prince*
Thomas Robert Malthus's *An Essay on the Principle of Population*
Mahmood Mamdani's *Citizen and Subject: Contemporary Africa And The Legacy Of Late Colonialism*
Karl Marx's *Capital*
John Stuart Mill's *On Liberty*
John Stuart Mill's *Utilitarianism*
Hans Morgenthau's *Politics Among Nations*
Thomas Paine's *Common Sense*
Thomas Paine's *Rights of Man*
Thomas Piketty's *Capital in the Twenty-First Century*
Robert D. Putman's *Bowling Alone*
John Rawls's *Theory of Justice*
Jean-Jacques Rousseau's *The Social Contract*
Theda Skocpol's *States and Social Revolutions*
Adam Smith's *The Wealth of Nations*
Sun Tzu's *The Art of War*
Henry David Thoreau's *Civil Disobedience*
Thucydides's *The History of the Peloponnesian War*
Kenneth Waltz's *Theory of International Politics*
Max Weber's *Politics as a Vocation*
Odd Arne Westad's *The Global Cold War: Third World Interventions And The Making Of Our Times*

POSTCOLONIAL STUDIES

Roland Barthes's *Mythologies*
Frantz Fanon's *Black Skin, White Masks*
Homi K. Bhabha's *The Location of Culture*
Gustavo Gutiérrez's *A Theology of Liberation*
Edward Said's *Orientalism*
Gayatri Chakravorty Spivak's *Can the Subaltern Speak?*

The Macat Library By Discipline

PSYCHOLOGY

Gordon Allport's *The Nature of Prejudice*
Alan Baddeley & Graham Hitch's *Aggression: A Social Learning Analysis*
Albert Bandura's *Aggression: A Social Learning Analysis*
Leon Festinger's *A Theory of Cognitive Dissonance*
Sigmund Freud's *The Interpretation of Dreams*
Betty Friedan's *The Feminine Mystique*
Michael R. Gottfredson & Travis Hirschi's *A General Theory of Crime*
Eric Hoffer's *The True Believer: Thoughts on the Nature of Mass Movements*
William James's *Principles of Psychology*
Elizabeth Loftus's *Eyewitness Testimony*
A. H. Maslow's *A Theory of Human Motivation*
Stanley Milgram's *Obedience to Authority*
Steven Pinker's *The Better Angels of Our Nature*
Oliver Sacks's *The Man Who Mistook His Wife For a Hat*
Richard Thaler & Cass Sunstein's *Nudge: Improving Decisions About Health, Wealth and Happiness*
Amos Tversky's *Judgment under Uncertainty: Heuristics and Biases*
Philip Zimbardo's *The Lucifer Effect*

SCIENCE

Rachel Carson's *Silent Spring*
William Cronon's *Nature's Metropolis: Chicago And The Great West*
Alfred W. Crosby's *The Columbian Exchange*
Charles Darwin's *On the Origin of Species*
Richard Dawkin's *The Selfish Gene*
Thomas Kuhn's *The Structure of Scientific Revolutions*
Geoffrey Parker's *Global Crisis: War, Climate Change and Catastrophe in the Seventeenth Century*
Mathis Wackernagel & William Rees's *Our Ecological Footprint*

SOCIOLOGY

Michelle Alexander's *The New Jim Crow: Mass Incarceration in the Age of Colorblindness*
Gordon Allport's *The Nature of Prejudice*
Albert Bandura's *Aggression: A Social Learning Analysis*
Hanna Batatu's *The Old Social Classes And The Revolutionary Movements Of Iraq*
Ha-Joon Chang's *Kicking Away the Ladder*
W. E. B. Du Bois's *The Souls of Black Folk*
Émile Durkheim's *On Suicide*
Frantz Fanon's *Black Skin, White Masks*
Frantz Fanon's *The Wretched of the Earth*
Eric Foner's *Reconstruction: America's Unfinished Revolution, 1863-1877*
Eugene Genovese's *Roll, Jordan, Roll: The World the Slaves Made*
Jack Goldstone's *Revolution and Rebellion in the Early Modern World*
Antonio Gramsci's *The Prison Notebooks*
Richard Herrnstein & Charles A Murray's *The Bell Curve: Intelligence and Class Structure in American Life*
Eric Hoffer's *The True Believer: Thoughts on the Nature of Mass Movements*
Jane Jacobs's *The Death and Life of Great American Cities*
Robert Lucas's *Why Doesn't Capital Flow from Rich to Poor Countries?*
Jay Macleod's *Ain't No Makin' It: Aspirations and Attainment in a Low Income Neighborhood*
Elaine May's *Homeward Bound: American Families in the Cold War Era*
Douglas McGregor's *The Human Side of Enterprise*
C. Wright Mills's *The Sociological Imagination*

Thomas Piketty's *Capital in the Twenty-First Century*
Robert D. Putman's *Bowling Alone*
David Riesman's *The Lonely Crowd: A Study of the Changing American Character*
Edward Said's *Orientalism*
Joan Wallach Scott's *Gender and the Politics of History*
Theda Skocpol's *States and Social Revolutions*
Max Weber's *The Protestant Ethic and the Spirit of Capitalism*

THEOLOGY

Augustine's *Confessions*
Benedict's *Rule of St Benedict*
Gustavo Gutiérrez's *A Theology of Liberation*
Carole Hillenbrand's *The Crusades: Islamic Perspectives*
David Hume's *Dialogues Concerning Natural Religion*
Immanuel Kant's *Religion within the Boundaries of Mere Reason*
Ernst Kantorowicz's *The King's Two Bodies: A Study in Medieval Political Theology*
Søren Kierkegaard's *The Sickness Unto Death*
C. S. Lewis's *The Abolition of Man*
Saba Mahmood's *The Politics of Piety: The Islamic Revival and the Feminist Subject*
Baruch Spinoza's *Ethics*
Keith Thomas's *Religion and the Decline of Magic*

Macat Disciplines

Access the greatest ideas and thinkers across entire disciplines, including

MACAT

AFRICANA STUDIES

Chinua Achebe's *An Image of Africa: Racism in Conrad's Heart of Darkness*

W. E. B. Du Bois's *The Souls of Black Folk*

Zora Neale Hurston's *Characteristics of Negro Expression*

Martin Luther King Jr.'s *Why We Can't Wait*

Toni Morrison's *Playing in the Dark: Whiteness in the American Literary Imagination*

Macat analyses are available from all good bookshops and libraries.

Access hundreds of analyses through one, multimedia tool.

Macat Disciplines

Access the greatest ideas and thinkers across entire disciplines, including

FEMINISM, GENDER AND QUEER STUDIES

Simone De Beauvoir's
The Second Sex

Michel Foucault's
History of Sexuality

Betty Friedan's
The Feminine Mystique

Saba Mahmood's
*The Politics of Piety:
The Islamic Revival and
the Feminist Subject*

Joan Wallach Scott's
*Gender and the
Politics of History*

Mary Wollstonecraft's
*A Vindication of the
Rights of Woman*

Virginia Woolf's
A Room of One's Own

Judith Butler's
Gender Trouble

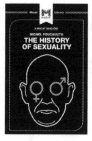

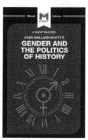

Macat analyses are available from all good bookshops and libraries.

Access hundreds of analyses through one, multimedia tool.
Join free for one month **library.macat.com**

Macat Disciplines

Access the greatest ideas and thinkers across entire disciplines, including

INEQUALITY

Ha-Joon Chang's, *Kicking Away the Ladder*

David Graeber's, *Debt: The First 5000 Years*

Robert E. Lucas's, *Why Doesn't Capital Flow from Rich To Poor Countries?*

Thomas Piketty's, *Capital in the Twenty-First Century*

Amartya Sen's, *Inequality Re-Examined*

Mahbub Ul Haq's, *Reflections on Human Development*

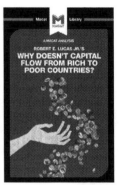

Macat analyses are available from all good bookshops and libraries.

Access hundreds of analyses through one, multimedia tool.

Join free for one month **library.macat.com**

Macat Disciplines

*Access the greatest ideas and thinkers
across entire disciplines, including*

CRIMINOLOGY

Michelle Alexander's
*The New Jim Crow:
Mass Incarceration in the
Age of Colorblindness*

**Michael R. Gottfredson
& Travis Hirschi's**
A General Theory of Crime

Elizabeth Loftus's
Eyewitness Testimony

**Richard Herrnstein
& Charles A. Murray's**
*The Bell Curve: Intelligence and
Class Structure in American Life*

Jay Macleod's
*Ain't No Makin' It:
Aspirations and Attainment in a
Low-Income Neighborhood*

Philip Zimbardo's
The Lucifer Effect

Macat Disciplines

Access the greatest ideas and thinkers across entire disciplines, including

POSTCOLONIAL STUDIES

Roland Barthes's *Mythologies*
Frantz Fanon's *Black Skin, White Masks*
Homi K. Bhabha's *The Location of Culture*
Gustavo Gutiérrez's *A Theology of Liberation*
Edward Said's *Orientalism*
Gayatri Chakravorty Spivak's *Can the Subaltern Speak?*

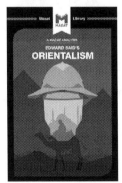

Macat analyses are available from all good bookshops and libraries.

Access hundreds of analyses through one, multimedia tool.

Join free for one month **library.macat.co**

Macat Disciplines

Access the greatest ideas and thinkers across entire disciplines, including

GLOBALIZATION

Arjun Appadurai's, *Modernity at Large: Cultural Dimensions of Globalisation*

James Ferguson's, *The Anti-Politics Machine*

Geert Hofstede's, *Culture's Consequences*

Amartya Sen's, *Development as Freedom*

Macat analyses are available from all good bookshops and libraries.

Access hundreds of analyses through one, multimedia tool.
Join free for one month **library.macat.com**

Macat Pairs

Analyse historical and modern issues from opposite sides of an argument. Pairs include:

HOW TO RUN AN ECONOMY

John Maynard Keynes's
The General Theory of Employment, Interest and Money

Classical economics suggests that market economies are self-correcting in times of recession or depression, and tend toward full employment and output. But English economist John Maynard Keynes disagrees.

In his ground-breaking 1936 study *The General Theory*, Keynes argues that traditional economics has misunderstood the causes of unemployment. Employment is not determined by the price of labor; it is directly linked to demand. Keynes believes market economies are by nature unstable, and so require government intervention. Spurred on by the social catastrophe of the Great Depression of the 1930s, he sets out to revolutionize the way the world thinks

Milton Friedman's
The Role of Monetary Policy

Friedman's 1968 paper changed the course of economic theory. In just 17 pages, he demolished existing theory and outlined an effective alternate monetary policy designed to secure 'high employment, stable prices and rapid growth.'

Friedman demonstrated that monetary policy plays a vital role in broader economic stability and argued that economists got their monetary policy wrong in the 1950s and 1960s by misunderstanding the relationship between inflation and unemployment. Previous generations of economists had believed that governments could permanently decrease unemployment by permitting inflation—and vice versa. Friedman's most original contribution was to show that this supposed trade-off is an illusion that only works in the short term.

Macat Pairs

*Analyse historical and modern issues
from opposite sides of an argument.
Pairs include:*

RACE AND IDENTITY

Zora Neale Hurston's
Characteristics of Negro Expression

Using material collected on anthropological
expeditions to the South, Zora Neale Hurston explains
how expression in African American culture in the
early twentieth century departs from the art of white
America. At the time, African American art was often
criticized for copying white culture. For Hurston, this
criticism misunderstood how art works. European
tradition views art as something fixed. But Hurston
describes a creative process that is alive, ever-
changing, and largely improvisational. She maintains
that African American art works through a process
called 'mimicry'—where an imitated object or verbal
pattern, for example, is reshaped and altered until
it becomes something new, novel—and worthy of
attention.

Frantz Fanon's
Black Skin, White Masks

Black Skin, White Masks offers a radical analysis of the
psychological effects of colonization on the colonized.

Fanon witnessed the effects of colonization first
hand both in his birthplace, Martinique, and again
later in life when he worked as a psychiatrist
in another French colony, Algeria. His text is
uncompromising in form and argument. He
dissects the dehumanizing effects of colonialism,
arguing that it destroys the native sense of identity,
forcing people to adapt to an alien set of values—
including a core belief that they are inferior. This
results in deep psychological trauma.

Fanon's work played a pivotal role in the civil rights
movements of the 1960s.

Macat analyses are available from all good bookshops and libraries.

Access hundreds of analyses through one, multimedia tool.
Join free for one month **library.macat.com**

Macat Pairs

Analyse historical and modern issues from opposite sides of an argument. Pairs include:

INTERNATIONAL RELATIONS IN THE 21ST CENTURY

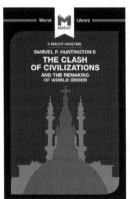

Samuel P. Huntington's
The Clash of Civilisations

In his highly influential 1996 book, Huntington offers a vision of a post-Cold War world in which conflict takes place not between competing ideologies but between cultures. The worst clash, he argues, will be between the Islamic world and the West: the West's arrogance and belief that its culture is a "gift" to the world will come into conflict with Islam's obstinacy and concern that its culture is under attack from a morally decadent "other."

Clash inspired much debate between different political schools of thought. But its greatest impact came in helping define American foreign policy in the wake of the 2001 terrorist attacks in New York and Washington.

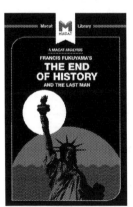

Francis Fukuyama's
The End of History and the Last Man

Published in 1992, *The End of History and the Last Man* argues that capitalist democracy is the final destination for all societies. Fukuyama believed democracy triumphed during the Cold War because it lacks the "fundamental contradictions" inherent in communism and satisfies our yearning for freedom and equality. Democracy therefore marks the endpoint in the evolution of ideology, and so the "end of history." There will still be "events," but no fundamental change in ideology.

Macat analyses are available from all good bookshops and libraries.

Access hundreds of analyses through one, multimedia tool.
Join free for one month **library.macat.com**

Macat Pairs

Analyse historical and modern issues from opposite sides of an argument. Pairs include:

ARE WE FUNDAMENTALLY GOOD - OR BAD?

Steven Pinker's
The Better Angels of Our Nature

Stephen Pinker's gloriously optimistic 2011 book argues that, despite humanity's biological tendency toward violence, we are, in fact, less violent today than ever before. To prove his case, Pinker lays out pages of detailed statistical evidence. For him, much of the credit for the decline goes to the eighteenth-century Enlightenment movement, whose ideas of liberty, tolerance, and respect for the value of human life filtered down through society and affected how people thought. That psychological change led to behavioral change—and overall we became more peaceful. Critics countered that humanity could never overcome the biological urge toward violence; others argued that Pinker's statistics were flawed.

Philip Zimbardo's
The Lucifer Effect

Some psychologists believe those who commit cruelty are innately evil. Zimbardo disagrees. In *The Lucifer Effect*, he argues that sometimes good people do evil things simply because of the situations they find themselves in, citing many historical examples to illustrate his point. Zimbardo details his 1971 Stanford prison experiment, where ordinary volunteers playing guards in a mock prison rapidly became abusive. But he also describes the tortures committed by US army personnel in Iraq's Abu Ghraib prison in 2003—and how he himself testified in defence of one of those guards. committed by US army personnel in Iraq's Abu Ghraib prison in 2003—and how he himself testified in defence of one of those guards.

Macat analyses are available from all good bookshops and libraries.

Access hundreds of analyses through one, multimedia tool.

Join free for one month **library.macat.com**

Macat Pairs

*Analyse historical and modern issues
from opposite sides of an argument.
Pairs include:*

HOW WE RELATE TO EACH OTHER AND SOCIETY

Jean-Jacques Rousseau's
The Social Contract

Rousseau's famous work sets out the radical concept of the 'social contract': a give-and-take relationship between individual freedom and social order.

If people are free to do as they like, governed only by their own sense of justice, they are also vulnerable to chaos and violence. To avoid this, Rousseau proposes, they should agree to give up some freedom to benefit from the protection of social and political organization. But this deal is only just if societies are led by the collective needs and desires of the people, and able to control the private interests of individuals. For Rousseau, the only legitimate form of government is rule by the people.

Robert D. Putnam's
Bowling Alone

In *Bowling Alone*, Robert Putnam argues that Americans have become disconnected from one another and from the institutions of their common life, and investigates the consequences of this change.

Looking at a range of indicators, from membership in formal organizations to the number of invitations being extended to informal dinner parties, Putnam demonstrates that Americans are interacting less and creating less "social capital" – with potentially disastrous implications for their society.

It would be difficult to overstate the impact of *Bowling Alone*, one of the most frequently cited social science publications of the last half-century.

Macat analyses are available from all good bookshops and libraries.

Access hundreds of analyses through one, multimedia tool.

Join free for one month **library.macat.com**

Printed in the United States
by Baker & Taylor Publisher Services